History First

1500 – 1750

Contents

1455	1460	1470	1480	1490	1500	1509

1455	1461	1483	1485	1486	1487	1489
First Battle of St Albans	Edward of York becomes king	Death of Edward IV. Richard of Gloucester becomes king	Henry Tudor becomes Henry VII	Henry marries Elizabeth of York	Prince Arthur born	Yorkshire rebellion

A day that **changed** English history?

The Battle of Bosworth Field

22 August 1485 was an important day in English history. On that day the Battle of Bosworth took place. Some historians have argued it was so important that it changed the course of English history...

Richard III was king of England in 1485. Richard was a member of the House of York. But there were still many nobles in England who supported the Lancastrians. These two groups had been fighting each other since 1455 in what became known as the Wars of the Roses. In 1485 the leader of the House of Lancaster was Henry Tudor. He wanted to take the throne from Richard.

Henry Tudor sailed from France and landed in England on 7 August 1485. With him he had an army of about 2,000 French **mercenaries** and a few Lancastrian knights and lords. As he marched across the country about 3,000 more men joined him. But his army was still heavily outnumbered when they met King Richard's 8,000 strong force. This was near the town of Market Bosworth in Leicestershire.

SOURCE A

A painting of Richard III's attack on Henry Tudor

4

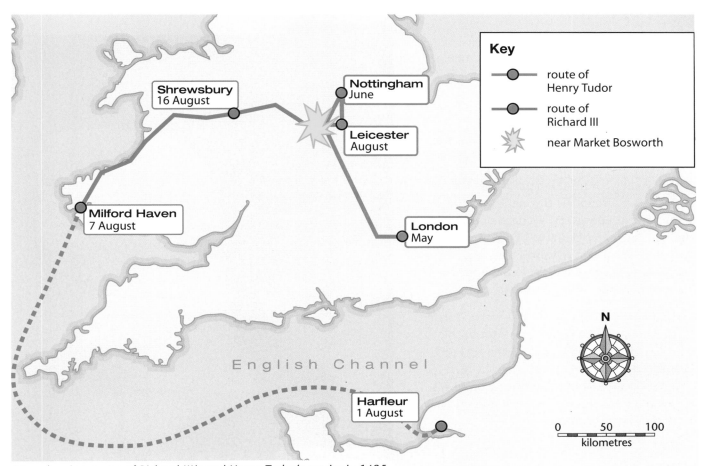

Map showing routes of Richard III's and Henry Tudor's armies in 1485

Richard should have won the battle, but two of the most powerful lords in his army did not support him. The Duke of Northumberland and his men took no part in the battle. Lord Stanley, who led 3,000 men and was Henry Tudor's stepfather, also refused to attack at first.

After the fighting started Richard noticed that only a few knights were guarding Henry Tudor. He saw an opportunity to attack. Richard led the charge himself and killed Henry's **standard bearer**. Next he beat down a huge knight who was trying to defend Henry. But it was too late. Lord Stanley had been watching the fight. He decided to help Henry not Richard. His men swept down to surround the king. Richard was knocked from his horse and died fighting bravely on foot. He is said to have shouted 'Treason, treason, treason' as he was killed.

Richard was only 32 years old when he died. He was the last English king to die in battle. The soldiers who killed him stripped his body, and two days later it was displayed in a local churchyard. The story goes that Richard's crown was found on the battlefield and Lord Stanley placed it on Henry Tudor's head.

ACTIVITIES

1. Why do you think Richard lost the Battle of Bosworth?

2. Why do you think Richard shouted 'treason' as he was killed?

3. Why do you think some historians have argued that the Battle of Bosworth changed the course of English history?

NEW WORDS

Mercenaries
soldiers who fight on any side in exchange for money

Standard bearer
the person who carries the flag

Securing the **Tudor dynasty...**
Why did Henry VII survive?

Henry Tudor was not the obvious choice of king in 1485. Despite his victory over Richard III at the Battle of Bosworth, his position was never really secure.

His claim to the throne came through his mother, Lady Margaret Beaufort. She was the great-great- granddaughter of Edward III.

Neither Henry VII nor Richard III had the most direct claim to the throne. It was the young sons of Edward IV, Richard's brother, who had the better claim. When Edward IV died, Richard said Edward's sons were illegitimate. They were locked away in the Tower of London – and never seen again!

Throughout his reign Henry was worried that the throne would be taken from him in the same way that he had seized it from Richard III. And yet he survived, and when he died in 1509 he was able to pass the throne on to his son, who became Henry VIII, unopposed. The Tudor **dynasty** was secure.

This is how Polydore Vergil, an Italian diplomat at Henry VII's court, explained his survival.

SOURCE A

Portrait of Henry VII

SOURCE B

'His spirit was wise; his mind was brave and never in the moments of the greatest danger, deserted him. In government he was clever, so that no one dared to get the better of him.'

But was Henry really clever, or was he just lucky?

ACTIVITIES

1. Look at the portrait of Henry VII in Source A. What impression does it give you of him? Does this agree with what you already know of him?

2. Polydore Vergil was a friend of Henry VII. How might this affect the usefulness of Source B?

3. Source B was written just after Henry's death. In what ways might this affect its usefulness?

NEW WORDS

Dynasty
a family of rulers

Pretenders
people who claim a right to the throne that many people don't accept

Truce
an agreement between enemies to stop fighting

Luck or **good judgement?**

FACT 1: MARRIAGE

In 1486 Henry married Elizabeth of York. Elizabeth was the daughter of Edward IV. This reunited the houses of York and Lancaster.

FACT 2: PEACE

After the Wars of the Roses the country wanted order, peace and stability.

FACT 3: PRETENDERS

During his reign Henry had to deal with two **pretenders** to his throne. Both said they were the sons of Edward IV – the Princes in the Tower. Henry defeated both.

FACT 4: SUCCESSION

Edward IV had two sons, but neither became king after him. When Henry VII died in 1509 he had a son who was old enough and able enough to become king.

FACT 5: RELATIONS WITH SCOTLAND

In 1486 Henry made a three year **truce** with King James III of Scotland. Henry later married his daughter Margaret to James IV.

FACT 6: RELATIONS WITH SPAIN

Henry arranged a marriage between his heir, Arthur, and a Spanish princess, Catherine of Aragon. They were married in 1501, but Arthur died in 1502. It was agreed that Catherine of Aragon would marry Arthur's younger brother, Henry.

FACT 7: FINANCE

Henry kept a close eye on finances. He managed crown lands well and raised lots of money from them. He also increased income from taxes and fines, and he avoided spending money on wars.

FACT 8: NOBLES

The nobles had become more powerful and wealthy. Many had private armies. Henry used the law to control these families. He imposed very heavy fines on those who broke the law.

ACTIVITIES

1 Which of the facts above suggest that Henry VII survived because:
   a) he was clever
   b) he was lucky
   c) neither of these?

Copy and complete the table below to record your decisions. The first one has been done for you. You may want to put some facts under more than one heading.

clever	lucky	neither
Fact 1		

2 Do you now think that Henry VII survived because he was: clever, lucky, or a combination of the two? Write a paragraph to explain your answer.

3 How was Henry VII able to secure the Tudor dynasty?

4 Did the Battle of Bosworth Field change the course of English history, or was it the actions of Henry VII?

Look back

Did you study Henry II in Year 7? Can you remember how he dealt with the nobles who had become too powerful after a period of civil war? Can you find any similarities with Henry VII?

1491	1500	1510	1520	1530

1491	1509	1520	1527	Jan 1533
Birth of Henry	Henry becomes king, marries Catherine of Aragon	The Field of the Cloth of Gold	Henry asks the Pope for a divorce from Catherine of Aragon	Henry marries Anne Boleyn

1509 – 1547

Henry the Great: image or reality?

The Field of the Cloth of Gold

Henry met Francis I, King of France, near Calais in 1520. They were there to make a lasting peace between the two countries. The meeting became known as the Field of the Cloth of Gold. This was because of the expensive cloth used to make some of the thousands of tents where the nobles slept.

For two weeks there were jousting competitions, banquets, balls and other exciting events. Henry VIII and Francis I wrestled each other. In the match Henry was thrown, but later he got his own back when he won an archery contest.

👁 ACTIVITIES

1. Henry VIII appears three times in this painting. He can be seen riding, **jousting** and greeting the French king. Can you find him?

2. Can you also spot:
   a) a fountain with taps for white, red and sweet wine
   b) a palace made of wood and canvas painted to look like brick
   c) two men who appear to be drunk on free wine
   d) a firework dragon
   e) cannons firing a salute?

The Field of The Cloth of Gold, painted in the mid-sixteenth century

Henry wanted to show he was just as powerful as the French king. To be seen as a great king he knew he had to spend money. The whole event cost Henry £15,000. That is £4.5 million in today's money. Of this, £2.5 million was spent on food and wine, and that was just the English share of the costs. It took the French 10 years to pay for theirs.

So what did all this expensive display of friendship lead to? The answer is, nothing much. Within three years England and France were at war again.

NEW WORDS

Jousting
    a fight between knights on horses with lances

ACTIVITIES

1. Why do you think Henry went to so much trouble to organise such a grand event?

2. Do you think it was wise to spend so much money in this way?

9

The truth about Henry VIII

Henry VIII is one of the most famous kings in British, and perhaps even world, history. Everything about him was 'big'. He had six wives – and executed two of them. He owned 60 palaces, 2,000 tapestries, almost 2,000 books and more than 90 swords. He dressed extravagantly and entertained lavishly. He destroyed over 500 monasteries and made himself Head of the Church in England. He spent vast amounts of money on wars and weapons, and portrayed himself as a warrior king. Nearly 72,000 people were executed during his 38 years on the throne. It is not surprising that he is remembered by history.

During the reign of his daughter Elizabeth I, Henry VIII was known as 'Great Harry' or 'Henry the Great'. But does he really deserve to be called 'Great', or was the image greater than the reality? What is the truth about Henry VIII?

Look back

What do you think makes a ruler 'great'? List your ideas. Look back to the section in *History First 1066–1500*, page 38, 'What did people expect of a medieval monarch?' for more ideas about what made a monarch great.

SOURCE A

This portrait of Henry VIII by a follower of Hans Holbein was painted in 1536. Holbein changed attitudes to portrait painting because his pictures were so lifelike and accurate. People began to use portraits to try and influence what people thought about them.

Finding out about Henry

At the end of this unit you are going to write a biography of Henry VIII. It will assess whether Henry deserved to be called 'Great'. You will need to think carefully about his strengths and weaknesses. You will be collecting information in a table and adding to it throughout the unit.

Evidence of greatness	Strengths	Weaknesses
First impressions		

What are your first impressions of Henry? Copy this table and then go over what you have read about Henry.

- Does the painting of the Field of the Cloth of Gold on pages 8–9 suggest Henry VIII was a great king? Explain your answer.
- What impression does Source A give you of Henry?

Born to **rule**?

You might expect that Henry spent his childhood preparing to be king. Not so. His older brother, Arthur, was to be the next king. But in 1502, Arthur died and Henry found himself heir to the kingdom of England.

When Henry VIII became king in 1509 he was just 17 years old. His **accession** to the throne was greeted with joy and hope. One noble, Lord Mountjoy, wrote:

> '...if you could see how all the world is rejoicing in possession of so great a prince.'

> But was Henry really 'so great a prince'? Can his upbringing and personality give any clues about whether he could become a great king?

Henry grew up during the Renaissance. This was a time during the fifteenth and sixteenth centuries when there was a huge interest in learning and the arts. Every ruler wanted a reputation for being strong and active, but also for being well educated and cultured.

There is no doubt that the young Henry was energetic and intelligent. **Venetian diplomat** Pasqualigo wrote in 1515:

> 'He speaks French, English and Latin, and a little Italian, plays well on the lute and harpsichord, sings songs from a book at sight, draws the bow with greater strength than any man in England, and jousts marvellously. Believe me, he is in every respect a most accomplished prince.'

Henry was also a forceful personality. He could be charming, affectionate and a bit of a romantic. But he was also known for flying into violent rages when he was angry. Henry hated failure and would throw tantrums and sulk. He could also be ruthless and cruel.

ACTIVITIES

1. Why did Henry become king?
2. Do you think there were any advantages or disadvantages in becoming king in this way? Give some reasons for your answer.

Henry could play most musical instruments, he wrote music and poetry, and read widely. He also loved playing bowls and tennis and he enjoyed wrestling, hunting and hawking.

NEW WORDS

- **Accession**
  becoming king or queen
- **Venetian diplomat**
  represented the government of Venice

Finding out about Henry

Does the young Henry sound like a great king to you? Think about what you have learned in this section about Henry's education, skills and personality. Any evidence of greatness should be added to the Strengths column. Anything that suggests he might not become a great king should be included in the Weaknesses column.

Evidence of greatness	Strengths	Weaknesses
First impressions		
The young Henry		

Did Henry **rule, or just reign?**

Henry VIII's government

Henry was the first English king for almost 100 years who hadn't had to win a battle to become king, or worry about someone stealing his crown. Unlike his father Henry VII, he was not a **usurper**.

Whilst Henry VII had a reputation for managing every detail of government, his son clearly enjoyed the good life. For nearly 25 years of Henry's 38-year reign, Cardinal Wolsey and, later, Thomas Cromwell had leading roles in running the country.

> So, did Henry rule, or just reign? Let's examine the role of Cardinal Wolsey to find out.

The glorious peacock: Cardinal Wolsey

Thomas Wolsey was Henry's 'chief minister' for 16 years. His story is one of 'rags to riches'. He was born in 1472, the son of a butcher in Ipswich. He went to Oxford University and became a priest. He was very ambitious, and looked for powerful friends. He used his connections to gain a place on the **privy council**. By 1514 he had been promoted to the position of Archbishop of York, and in 1515 he became Lord Chancellor and **Cardinal**. Until his fall in 1529 he was effectively Henry's chief minister.

Thomas Wolsey in his Cardinal's robes

But there was another side to the 'glorious peacock'. As a young man he had lived with an inn-keeper's daughter, and had two children with her. As Cardinal, he became rich by taking bribes. By 1520, the butcher's son from Ipswich lived in palaces. He gave magnificent feasts, but he always ate alone, sitting under a cloth of state like the king. He dressed in silk, and carried an orange filled with a sponge of vinegar to keep off the smell of the poor. And he always kept visitors waiting!

It was Wolsey who built Hampton Court Palace. It rivalled the King's palaces in its size and splendour

In 1519 the Venetian ambassador had told his government that Wolsey 'is the person who rules both the King and the entire Kingdom.' But was this really true?

Henry left much of the day-to-day running of the government to Wolsey, whilst he danced, dined, jousted or hunted. Wolsey had enormous influence over Henry. He advised him on policies and sometimes made his own. Some historians think their relationship was more of a partnership than master–servant.

In the things Henry was interested in, like foreign policy, he was far more involved. Visiting foreign ambassadors always found him very knowledgeable. Unfortunately for Wolsey, this meant dealing with Henry's ambitions to conquer France. This cost a lot of money.

Wolsey's attempts to raise more taxes started a rebellion in East Anglia. Even though he was just doing his job, Wolsey got all the blame! To keep Henry happy, Wolsey gave him Hampton Court Palace. Wolsey always knew his power was dependent on Henry's goodwill. Henry shared his crown with no one. When Wolsey failed to deliver Henry his divorce from Catherine of Aragon, Henry's favour finally ran out. In 1529 Henry had Wolsey arrested on treason charges. He died on the way to face trial in London, a broken man.

Over the next few pages you will find out why Henry wanted to divorce Catherine and why it was so difficult.

NEW WORDS

Cardinal
very important person in the Catholic church, appointed by the Pope

Privy Council
a group of people appointed by the king to advise him

Usurper
someone who has seized or 'stolen' the throne, without having a right to it

ACTIVITIES

1. Why do you think Wolsey was nicknamed the 'glorious peacock'?

2. Do you think Wolsey was:
   a) a man of God
   b) a man 'on the make'
   c) a loyal servant to Henry VIII
   d) a combination of **a–c**?

   Give some reasons for your answer.

3. Do you think Wolsey:
   a) was in control of government policy
   b) carried out Henry's wishes in government
   c) was allowed to get on with governing the country as long as Henry was in agreement?

Look back

Do you remember the other Thomas at the court of Henry II? Look back to *History First 1066–1500*, pages 54–59, at the career of Thomas Becket. Are there any similarities between Thomas Becket and Thomas Wolsey?

Finding out about Henry

What evidence is there in this section that Henry was a great king? Think about your answers to activities 2 and 3 above and try to add to your table.

Evidence of greatness	Strengths	Weaknesses
First impressions		
The young Henry		
Control of government and policy		

Defend the faith, or find an heir?

The King's great matter

Henry married Catherine of Aragon in 1509. Their marriage seems to have been a happy one, lasting over 20 years. Like Henry, Catherine loved hunting, music and dancing. She and Henry discussed politics, religion and books together. Yet by 1527 Henry was trying to divorce her. Why?

Catherine of Aragon

NEW WORDS

Adultery
having sex with a person when married to someone else

Heir
the person, usually a son, who will take over on the death of a monarch

Legitimate
the child of parents who are married

Stillborn
a child born dead

Succession
the question of who should be the next monarch

> We have had four children. Two were **stillborn** and our son died within a year. Only our daughter Mary has survived. Catherine is unlikely to have any more children.

> The last time that England was ruled by a woman there was a civil war (Queen Matilda, 1135). I need a male **heir** to ensure a safe **succession**.

> Catherine is five years older than me. She is fat and isn't attractive any more. I've taken mistresses – in 1519 one of them gave birth to a son. Perhaps God is punishing me for marrying my brother's widow by not giving me a **legitimate** son.

Henry was 45 years old when Hans Holbein painted this portrait in 1536

14

Anne Boleyn

'Madame Anne is not one of the handsomest women in the world. She is of middling stature, long neck, wide mouth, bosom not much raised, and in fact has nothing but the King's great appetite – and her eyes, which are black and beautiful.'

Written by an Italian visitor to Henry's court

Anne was 10 years younger than Henry. She was crowned queen in 1533 but she was not popular with most English people. In 1536, just three years later, Henry had her arrested on a charge of witchcraft and **adultery**. She was found guilty and sentenced to death. A special executioner was brought over from France. He used a sword to make Anne's death quicker. It is said that Anne's eyes continued to blink even after her head was cut off. Henry declared their marriage had never been valid and their daughter Elizabeth was illegitimate. Only days after Anne's death he married again.

ACTIVITIES

1. What were Henry's *religious* reasons for wanting a divorce from Catherine? Explain your answer.

2. What were Henry's *political* reasons for wanting a divorce from Catherine? Explain your answer.

3. What were Henry's *personal* reasons for wanting a divorce from Catherine? Explain your answer.

> I met Anne Boleyn in 1526 and I've fallen in love with her. But she won't sleep with me unless we're married!

> Catherine used to be married to my brother Arthur. Even though they didn't sleep together, my father needed special permission from the Pope to allow me to marry her. The Church disapproves of marriages between relatives.

Finding out about Henry

Think about what you have learned about Henry in this section. You will need to think very carefully here, as there are lots of different issues, but they all get mixed up in the 'King's Great Matter'.

- What were his main reasons for wanting a divorce?

- What does this tell you about what Henry thought his most important duties as king were?

- Can you find any evidence of greatness?

Add 'The King's Great Matter' to the Evidence of greatness column in your table and record your ideas.

The break with Rome

To divorce Catherine, Henry needed the Pope's permission. Henry knew this would be difficult. The Pope was the head of the Catholic Church, which disagreed with divorce. What would Henry do?

Strategy 1: Persuading the Pope

Henry asked Cardinal Wolsey to convince the Pope of his case. Unfortunately, the Pope was virtually a prisoner of Charles V, King of Spain and nephew of Catherine of Aragon. Wolsey's negotiations failed.

Instead the Pope sent an envoy to help Henry patch up the marriage. When that failed, he tried to persuade Catherine to become a nun. She refused. So in 1529 a special court was set up to examine the case. When Henry arrived, Catherine threw herself at his feet and begged him to think again about divorcing her.

Catherine left the room and refused to return. Instead, she appealed to Charles V, who forced the Pope to end the court case. Furious, Henry sent Catherine away from Hampton Court and stopped her from seeing their daughter, Mary.

Strategy 2: Attacking the Church

Meanwhile, criticism of the Catholic Church was growing. Some people said that church leaders were not leading the holy and simple lives they were supposed to. Others argued that the Church had grown too rich and powerful, and that the Pope had more power in England than the king. Some thought that the king should take charge of reforming the Church.

Henry was looking for a new strategy. An adviser called Thomas Cromwell encouraged the King to use Parliament to reduce the Pope's power in England. Henry hoped this would put pressure on the Pope. The Pope hit back, threatening to **excommunicate** Henry.

Then in December 1532, Anne became pregnant. Henry was convinced she would have a boy. It was now a race against time to secure the divorce so that he could marry Anne and have a legitimate heir.

Catherine's appeal to Henry. A nineteenth century painting

Strategy 3: Making the break

Anne and Henry were secretly married in January 1533. Drastic action was now necessary. Henry realised that if he were in charge of the Church, he could force the bishops to grant him his divorce. It was a revolutionary idea. No one but the Pope had ever been head of the Church.

Parliament was called and laws were passed cutting the links between Rome and the English Church. A special court decided that Catherine's marriage to Henry had never been valid. In May 1533 Anne Boleyn was crowned queen.

ACTIVITIES

1 Which of the following do you think was the main reason for the break with Rome? Was it:

   a) failings within the Catholic Church

   b) Henry's love for Anne Boleyn

   c) Henry's need for a male heir

   d) Henry's belief that his marriage to Catherine of Aragon had been against God's wishes

   e) Henry wanting to control the Church himself

   f) A combination of the above?

   Explain your answer.

2 Why do you think Henry was prepared to upset so many people?

3 Why do you think Henry treated those who opposed him so harshly?

NEW WORDS

Excommunicate
   remove from church membership

A step too far?

But Henry didn't stop there. He made himself Supreme Governor of the English Church. Henry made all the important men in the kingdom swear an oath to accept him as head of the Church.

But some could not bring themselves to do this. Thomas More, Henry's Lord Chancellor, refused to swear the oath. He was arrested and executed. In 1535 five churchmen who refused to swear the oath were executed as traitors. The arm of one man was left hanging over his monastery's door. Several monks were left to die in a London dungeon. They were chained and loaded down with lead so they could not stand up.

Henry had got what he wanted. But he had upset a lot of people in the process. His marriage to Anne was never popular, and many resented the religious changes he had made.

Monks being drawn to their execution for opposing Henry

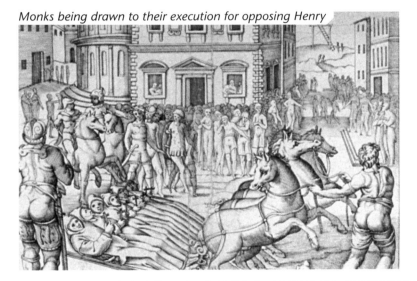

Finding out about Henry

It's time to add to your table again. You have probably realised by now that Henry was not quite what he seemed. Think about your answers to all the activities in this section:

- Think of at least three adjectives that describe Henry's approach to getting a divorce.

- What do these tell you about Henry's character?

- Do you think Henry's actions were those of a great king? If not, why not?

Add 'The Break with Rome' to the Evidence of greatness column and add details to the Strengths and Weaknesses columns.

Faith or **finance?**

What happened to the monasteries?

In 1535, religious houses – monasteries, nunneries and priories – were a very important part of life. There were over 500 in England and Wales, providing hospitality to travellers, care to the sick and homes to more than 10,000 monks, friars and nuns. They were also very rich. They owned over a quarter of all the farmed land in England. Yet by 1540 all the religious houses had been closed down. Why did this happen?

After he fell out with the Pope, Henry began to see the church in England, and especially the monks and nuns, as a major source of opposition. In 1536 Cromwell, at Henry's bidding, sent out royal **commissioners** to investigate all the monasteries and nunneries in England. They reported that many monks and nuns were not living holy lives.

Rievaulx Abbey today

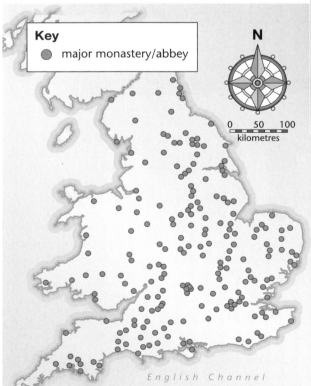

Key
● major monastery/abbey

N

0   50   100
kilometres

English Channel

Map of England and Wales, showing the most important monasteries and abbeys before 1536

Examples of **immorality**, such as adultery, drunkenness, failure to pay debts and failure to care for travellers and the poor, were widespread. We cannot be sure how much of the report was true, but it gave Henry the excuse he needed. Most of the smaller monasteries were closed down in the following year.

By 1540 all the religious houses had been closed. The monks and priors who surrendered their houses to the King were given pensions or other jobs in the Church. In total about 8,000 monks were pensioned off. In some cases, they seem to have confessed to wrongdoings they could not have committed. The nuns were not so well treated and many of them ended up as servants or beggars. A few, who resisted closure, were executed like traitors.

Greed or greatness?

The King took all the monasteries' wealth, and much of their land was sold off. Wagonloads of jewels were taken away. Lead was removed from roofs and windows. Even stone was taken for building works elsewhere. Henry suddenly had a lot more money than before. The Crown's income had doubled.

But there was a huge cost. Many magnificent church buildings were destroyed and books (illuminated manuscripts), images and **reliquaries** were lost in the **dissolution** of the monasteries.

In many areas these changes were accepted, or even supported, but in the north of England a massive revolt broke out in October 1536. This was known as the Pilgrimage of Grace. People were opposed to the religious changes. They wanted to keep the monasteries. It was the most serious threat to Henry's reign yet. At first Henry pretended to give in and the revolt ended peacefully. But when Henry was ready he struck back and over 200 people were executed.

ACTIVITIES

1. What do you think was the purpose of the investigation of all religious houses in 1536?

2. How was the dissolution of the monasteries justified?

3. What do you think was the real reason for the dissolution of the monasteries? Was it:
   a) an attempt to reform a corrupt Church
   b) a means of gaining money for the Crown
   c) a combination of these?

   Write a short paragraph to explain your answer.

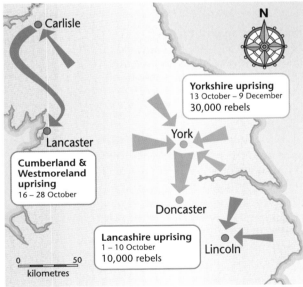

Map of northen England, showing the route of the rebels

'The northern men ... had assembled themselves into a huge and great army of warlike men, well appointed with captains, horse, armour and artillery, to the number of 40,000 men, who had encamped themselves in Yorkshire.'

Edward Hall described the revolt in 1536

Finding out about Henry

What have you learned about Henry in this section?

- What does the dissolution tell you about his motives? Think about your answer to activity 3 above.

- Do you think he was a clever politician?

What do you think? Add 'The Dissolution of the Monasteries' to the Evidence of greatness column on your table and record your ideas about Henry's strengths and weaknesses.

Fighting the French, finite and fortifications

Henry's foreign policy

When Henry VIII became king in 1509, England was not a powerful country in Europe. His father Henry VII had very carefully avoided being dragged into wars. Unusually, when Henry VIII became king, the Crown was not in debt.

Henry wanted to be a 'warrior king', to rival Francis I, King of France, and Charles V, the Holy Roman Emperor. He dreamt of winning back the title of King of France, which every English king since Edward III had claimed. He spent a lot of money and energy fighting wars with, or trying to impress, the French. (Remember the painting of the Field of the Cloth of Gold?)

But despite his enthusiasm, his successes were limited. England's geographical position at the edge of Europe meant that she could not play a central role, and was sometimes at the mercy of events on the continent. Henry had discovered this to his cost during his divorce negotiations with the Pope.

Ireland
Henry claimed to be King of Ireland in 1541 but never established English control.

Wales
Henry made Wales fully part of England in 1536.

France
France was England's traditional enemy and Scotland's ally. To create an alliance, Henry married his younger sister Mary to the old French king Louis XII. However, when he died, Mary secretly married Henry's best friend, Charles Brandon. Henry was furious! He could no longer use Mary to make any more marriage alliances.

Henry fought three wars against the French in 1512–14, 1522–25 and 1543–46. He captured Boulogne in 1544. However, there was little else to show for all the fighting and huge sums of money spent.

Spain
When Henry became king, Spain was an ally, through his marriage to Catherine of Aragon. Henry's divorce and break with Rome damaged relations between the two countries.

For the rest of his reign, Henry was forced to deal with the threat of both Catholic France and Spain. Although they were usually fighting each other, on several occasions they allied together against England, as in 1538.

Map of western Europe during Henry's reign

Scotland

Scotland was a constant menace. Henry defeated the Scots at the Battle of Flodden in 1513 and at the Battle of Solway Moss in 1542. But he was never able to crush them. The Scots were allies of France.

Netherlands

Henry tried to keep strong links with the Netherlands, which was important to the English cloth trade. The Netherlands was controlled by the Holy Roman Emperor, Charles V.

NETHERLANDS

○ **Duchy of Cleves**

HOLY ROMAN EMPIRE

Holy Roman Empire

The Holy Roman Empire was a vast area, divided into hundreds of separate states. Its ruler was Charles V, who was also King of Spain. When England needed an ally against Catholic France and Spain in 1540, Henry was persuaded to marry Anne of Cleves, the daughter of the Protestant Duke of Cleves.

However, the alliance was short lived, as Henry divorced Anne (his fourth wife) within six months. After this, Henry found it difficult to find any foreign princess who would marry him.

| 0 | 100 | 200 | 300 | 400 | 500 |

kilometres

ACTIVITIES

1. Make a list of Henry's successes in foreign policy.

2. Do you think Henry VIII deserves to be described as a 'warrior king'?

3. Do you think England was a more powerful country in Europe at the end of Henry VIII's reign than she had been in 1509? Why do you think this?

4. Was Henry's foreign policy successful enough to justify the vast amount of money spent on it? Write a paragraph to explain your answer.

Finding out about Henry

Henry was particularly interested in foreign policy. He wanted to be as important as Charles V and Francis I. He failed in his biggest dream, to conquer France. Does this mean his foreign policy was unsuccessful?

Think about your answers to activities 2–4 above. What do you really think about Henry VIII's foreign policy?

Add 'Foreign Policy' to the Evidence of Greatness column of your table. Include any evidence of greatness in the Strengths column. Don't forget to record details that suggest he was not great in the Weaknesses column.

Henry's defensive policy

As a result of the break with Rome, the Pope had lost his power in England. He wanted a holy **crusade** against England to get this control back. He called upon Christians everywhere to attack Henry VIII.

The opportunity came in 1538. France and Spain had just signed a 10-year truce. They began to gather ships for an attack against Henry. For the first time in 300 years, England faced a serious threat of invasion.

Henry acted quickly. Ships patrolled the coast to watch for an invasion fleet. Chains of beacon fires were made ready to signal if enemy ships were sighted. Soldiers were **mustered**. Ditches were dug and barricades built.

A survey was made of places that needed extra defence. Next, a string of small castles was built close to beaches where troops could land, or near bays where invasion fleets could anchor. Most of these castles still survive today. Pendennis, St Mawes, Deal, Walmer and the others were a new type of fortress specially built to protect the coast. They were strongly made and designed to contain cannons. Henry took a personal interest in their construction and may even have helped with the designs. The money he gained from closing the monasteries helped to pay for these new castles, and in some cases they provided the stones too.

Henry was also responsible for a massive expansion of the navy. At first, **merchant ships** were armed to defend England. But he also ordered powerful new ships to be built, including the *Great Harry* and the *Mary Rose*. Some historians regard Henry VIII as the founder of the modern Royal Navy. Over 30 warships were built during his reign.

The threat of 1538 passed. No great enemy fleets tried to land invading soldiers to remove Henry from the throne. France and Spain were soon enemies again. But England was left far safer than it had been before.

However, the cost of defending England was huge. Henry had spent much of the money he had made from closing down the monasteries.

St Mawes Castle

Map of southern England, showing the castles built by Henry

The Mary Rose was built between 1509 and 1511, just after Henry became king. It was the pride of Henry's fleet. It was one of the first warships that could fire a **broadside** *at the enemy*

ACTIVITIES

1. Why did Henry have to spend so much money defending England?

2. How did Henry pay for his defensive policy?

3. Do you think Henry should be praised for strengthening England's defences? Why?

4. Do you think Henry should be criticised for following policies that threatened England's security? Explain your answer.

NEW WORDS

Broadside
firing all the canon on one side of a ship at the same time

Crusade
Holy war

Merchant ships
ships carrying goods

Mustered
Gathered to fight

Finding out about Henry

Think about what you have learned about Henry in this section, and your answers to the activities opposite.

- Which adjectives best describe Henry's response to the threat of invasion?

frightened	decisive	clever	rapid
slow	costly	necessary	pointless
worried	timid	half-hearted	wasteful

- Was he great because he made England far safer than before?

- Or was his defensive policy the result of an unwise foreign policy?

Add 'Defensive Policy' to the Evidence of greatness column in your table and record your ideas.

Henry's **final fling**

If you knew anything about Henry VIII before reading this chapter it was probably that he had six wives. From his marriage to Catherine he had a daughter, Mary, and from his marriage to Anne he had a second daughter, Elizabeth. In 1536, just after the execution of Anne Boleyn, Henry married his third wife, Jane Seymour, who finally provided him with the longed-for heir.

> At last Henry had a son. Yet he went on to marry three more times in the final 10 years of his reign. Why did he do this and what does it tell us about him?

In 1540 Henry married for the fourth time. His bride was Anne of Cleves.

Jane Seymour was a lady-in-waiting to Anne Boleyn. Jane helped bring Henry back into contact with his daughters. There was national rejoicing when Jane gave birth to a son, Edward, in 1537. But she died a few days later after a difficult birth.

Henry chose Anne of Cleves from a number of possible foreign princesses. He had not seen her when he proposed, but liked the way she looked in a portrait by Holbein. Henry was keen to make an alliance with Anne's father who was a powerful German prince. From their first meeting Henry did not find her attractive and soon sent her away. Just six months after the marriage they were divorced.

ACTIVITIES

1. Look at the portrait of Henry in Source A. What impression does it give you of him? Why?

2. Now look back at the portrait of Henry VIII on page 10. In what ways is it similar to or different from Source A?

3. Why do you think Henry married so many times? Give as many reasons as you can.

Finding out about Henry

1. What does the story of the six wives add to our understanding of Henry as a king?

- Was he great because he understood that it was his duty to form alliances with other countries and get an heir?
- Was he not a great king because he treated his wives badly?
- Or was he just unlucky with his marriages, so they do not affect whether he was great or not?

2. Add 'The six wives' to the Evidence of greatness column and record your ideas to complete the table.

Writing your biography

> Your research is now finished. It is time to use what you have found out to help you decide whether Henry VIII deserved to be known as 'Henry the Great'.

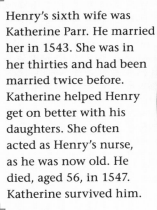

Catherine Howard was a cousin of Anne Boleyn. She was 16 when she married Henry in July 1540. He was 49. She was pretty and the king showered her with presents. When Catherine was discovered to be having an affair with her music teacher, she was arrested and beheaded in 1542. Henry was humiliated.

Henry's sixth wife was Katherine Parr. He married her in 1543. She was in her thirties and had been married twice before. Katherine helped Henry get on better with his daughters. She often acted as Henry's nurse, as he was now old. He died, aged 56, in 1547. Katherine survived him.

SOURCE A

This portrait was made when Henry was an old man. By the time of his marriage to Catherine Howard, Henry was not good-looking. He developed painful ulcers in his legs and found it hard to stand and walk. He became grossly fat and had to be winched upstairs.

1 Look at the information you have collected in your table. What do you now think made a ruler in the sixteenth century 'great'?

2 Write a list of your ideas. You might want to look back at your answer to the 'look back' activity on page 10.

You are going to write a biography of Henry VIII. A good biography tells someone's life story and analyses it. It looks at the way the person's life was remarkable, how their personality influenced what they did, and if they made any mistakes or bad decisions.

Here is a checklist, or toolkit, that might help you:

- **INTRODUCTION**

Write a short paragraph explaining why Henry is remembered and what image we have of him.

- **MAIN PART OF THE BIOGRAPHY**

Use the information in your table to write a paragraph for each of your ideas. Remember, you are explaining whether or not you think Henry deserves to be called great.

- **CONCLUSION**

Write a final paragraph in which you decide whether Henry does deserve to be called Henry the Great.

Palaces and pies

Hampton Court

Henry VIII believed that he had to show people he was a great king. One way that he did this was by displaying his wealth. He spent vast sums on new palaces and on entertaining the people at his court.

Hampton Court Palace

Henry owned more houses than any other English monarch. When he died he had more than 70 homes. Some were old castles, some were new palaces and some were smaller hunting lodges. Many of the new homes he built were near to the River Thames, so he could reach them by boat. Others were close to hunting parks.

The only palace that survives, much as it was when Henry was alive, is Hampton Court. It was the last Tudor palace built with a great hall. Here up to 300 people could sit down to eat. Two sittings were needed to feed the people at court. However, Henry usually ate in his privy (private) chamber.

For most people at court, breakfast was at 7am. They usually had bread, meat and ale.

The main meal was dinner. This was served between 10 am and 1 pm. There was supper in the evening and a snack before bedtime.

The number of dishes and type of food people at court ate depended on how important they were. On one occasion in 1517 Henry entertained a foreign ambassador with a ten course meal that lasted seven hours! Servants had cheap cuts of meat and **pottage**. The nobles at court would expect boiled or roast beef, pheasant, lamb, chicken and other meats, while for the most important there might be venison, swan, heron or peacock. To follow were fruit pies and tarts. Most fruit was served cooked. Eating raw fruit was thought to be unhealthy.

Hampton Court's kitchens

It would cost over £6 million a year to feed the court at today's prices. To go with all this food there was ale, and wine for the nobles. The 300 barrels of wine drunk every year added over £500,000 to the food bill.

Feeding all the people at court was a huge operation. In each palace there was a set of kitchens staffed by hundreds of workers. At Hampton Court the kitchens took up a third of the floor space in the palace. Fifty people worked, slept and ate in the Great Kitchen. There were also smaller kitchens and offices surrounding it. Staff in each room had a different job, making everything from sauces to bread. Over 200 loaves a day had to be baked to go with the meat. This was a time when there was no rice or potatoes, and vegetables were only just becoming popular. Previously vegetables were seen as food for the poor.

On the move

Organising the court in one palace was complicated enough, but Henry would regularly move between homes. Most of the furniture and many of the servants moved, too. Everything had to be taken apart, packed into wagons and re-assembled in the next palace. This included Henry's great bed with its eight mattresses. Henry even had a portable lock that was fitted to his bedroom door each time he moved.

Although Henry liked more privacy as he got older, he was never alone. The queen had separate apartments. If Henry wished to visit her at night he was escorted there, and escorted back later in the night. There were always servants sleeping outside his door and there was another at the foot of his bed.

👁 ACTIVITY

Foreign visitors were impressed by the music and entertainment at Henry's court. What do you think they said about the meals? Write down some details they might have put in their letters home.

NEW WORDS

Pottage
meat soup that might include oatmeal, vegetables and herbs

1483	1490	1500	1510	1520	1530	1540	1550	1553

1483	1505	1517	1533	1552	1553
Birth of Martin Luther	Luther becomes a monk	Luther's 95 Theses start the Reformation	Henry VIII's Break with Rome	A new Protestant Prayer Book is issued	The Pope becomes Head of the English Church again

Link 2

A beginning and an end:
the Reformation

On 31 October 1517, Martin Luther went to the Castle Church in Wittenberg. He did not go to worship or to admire. In his hands he carried a piece of paper and a hammer. At the door he stopped. He nailed the piece of paper on to the door and walked away. The Reformation had begun. The Church of the Middle Ages, with the Pope in Rome at its head, would never be the same again. How could this event, which seemed so insignificant, lead to such significant changes within the Church?

NEW WORDS

Nationalism
   wanting one's own country to be independent of others

Tithes
   people had to pay 10 per cent of their income to the church

Luther nailing his 95 Theses to the door of the Castle Church in Wittenberg

Martin Luther

Martin Luther was the son of a copper miner in Saxony, Germany. He was well educated. He decided to devote his life to God after being knocked down by lightning in a violent thunderstorm.

As a monk, Luther led a very strict life, often fasting and praying for days on end. In 1510 he was sent to Rome, the centre of the Roman Catholic Church. Here he was shocked by the wealth and wickedness of many of the churchmen. In 1511 Luther became a lecturer at the university in Wittenberg. Whilst preparing his lectures he began to question some of the teachings of the Church.

The essay that Luther nailed to the door of the Castle Church in Wittenberg in October 1517 gave 95 reasons why he disagreed with the Roman Catholic Church. It became known as the 95 Theses. His complaints were moderate, but many people agreed with them. Without his permission, the 95 Theses were copied and quickly spread across Germany and Europe.

Why did the Reformation spread?

The Reformation split the Church. Those who disagreed with the teachings of the Roman Catholic Church protested and became known as Protestants.

1 **It was a time of rising prices.** Many people hated having to pay **tithes** to the Church, especially as much of this money went out of the country to the Pope.

2 **The growth of nationalism.** Some people wanted the Church to belong to their own country, without interference from the Pope.

3 **People's lives were changing.** Merchants, shopkeepers and craftsmen in the towns wanted to make a profit and they did not like the power the Church had over their daily lives. Some kings and queens agreed with them.

4 **The Catholic Church was corrupt.** Many important people within the Church, including the Pope, used their positions to become very rich and powerful. They did not live godly lives.

5 **It was a time of general change.** It was the time of the Renaissance when accepted ideas in art and science were being challenged. It was also the time of the voyages of discovery. Everything, including religion, was being questioned.

6 **The development of printing.** This meant that the ideas of people who challenged the teachings of the Roman Catholic Church, became widely known – and supported.

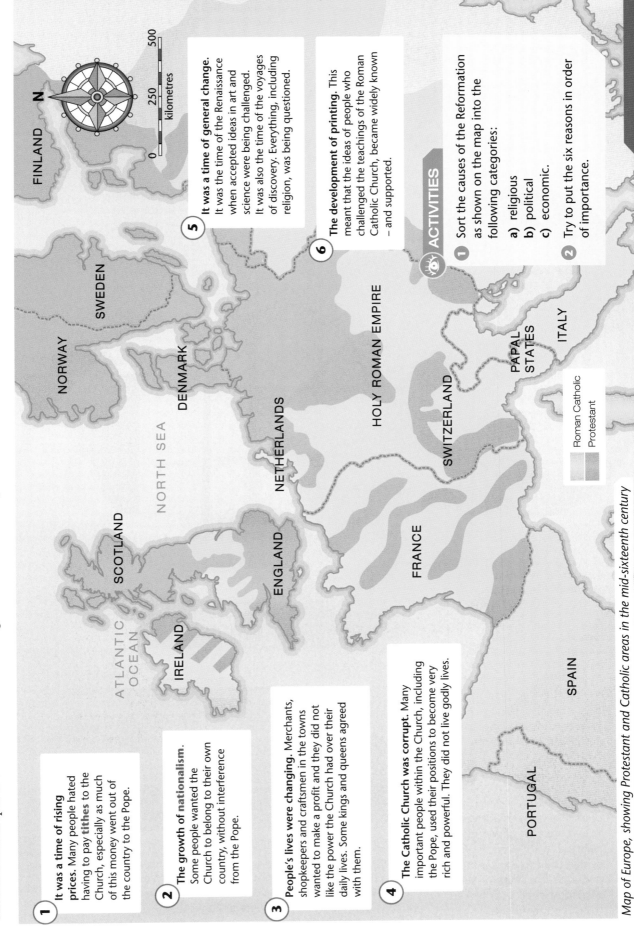

FINLAND

NORWAY

SWEDEN

DENMARK

NORTH SEA

NETHERLANDS

HOLY ROMAN EMPIRE

SWITZERLAND

ITALY

PAPAL STATES

FRANCE

ENGLAND

SCOTLAND

IRELAND

ATLANTIC OCEAN

SPAIN

PORTUGAL

MEDITERRANEAN SEA

Roman Catholic
Protestant

N

0   250   500
kilometres

Map of Europe, showing Protestant and Catholic areas in the mid-sixteenth century

ACTIVITIES

1 Sort the causes of the Reformation as shown on the map into the following categories:
  a) religious
  b) political
  c) economic.

2 Try to put the six reasons in order of importance.

Link 2

Henry's children:
the Reformation in England
Edward VI (reigned 1547–1553)

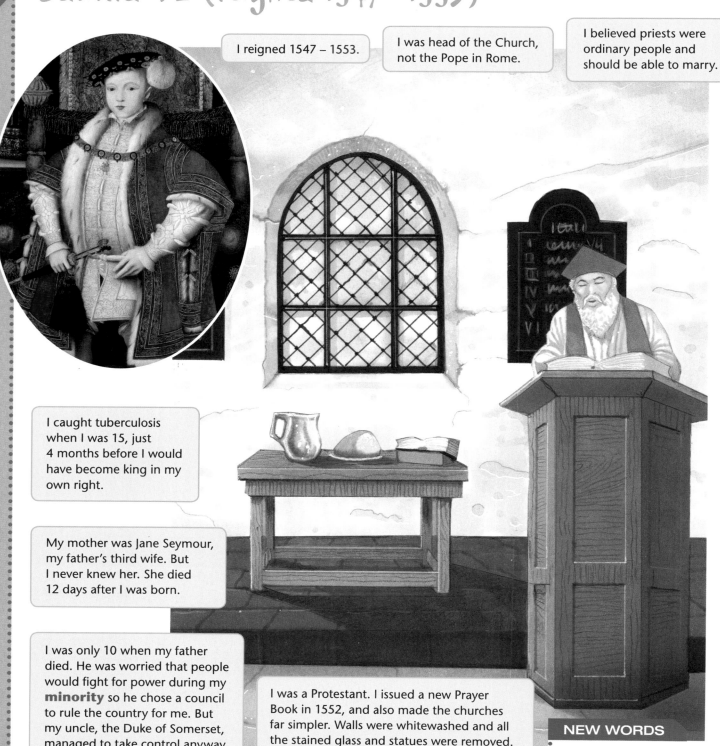

I reigned 1547 – 1553.

I was head of the Church, not the Pope in Rome.

I believed priests were ordinary people and should be able to marry.

I caught tuberculosis when I was 15, just 4 months before I would have become king in my own right.

My mother was Jane Seymour, my father's third wife. But I never knew her. She died 12 days after I was born.

I was only 10 when my father died. He was worried that people would fight for power during my **minority** so he chose a council to rule the country for me. But my uncle, the Duke of Somerset, managed to take control anyway. He was a Protestant.

I was a Protestant. I issued a new Prayer Book in 1552, and also made the churches far simpler. Walls were whitewashed and all the stained glass and statues were removed. The church services were in English.

NEW WORDS

Minority
period of being under age

Mary I (reigned 1553–1558)

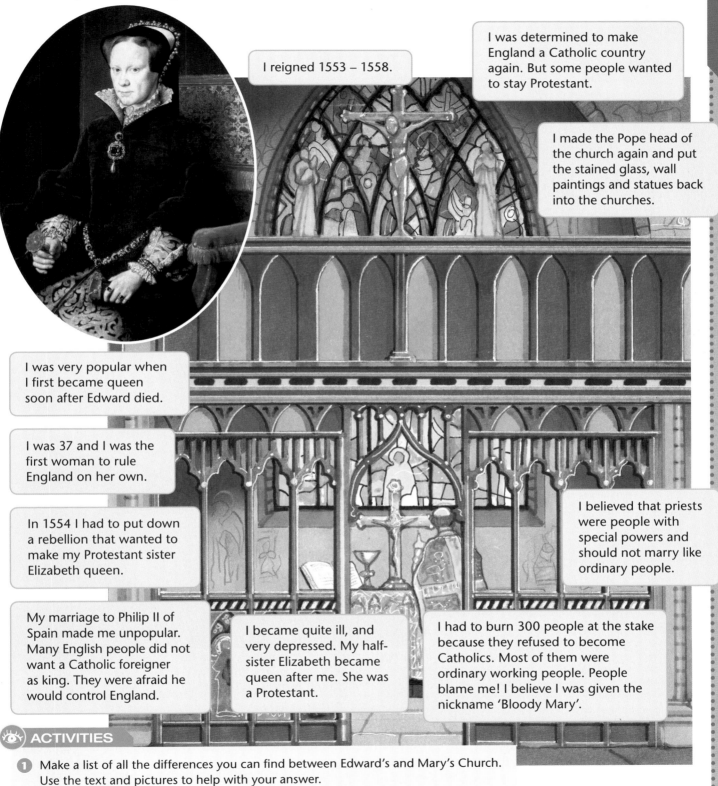

I reigned 1553 – 1558.

I was determined to make England a Catholic country again. But some people wanted to stay Protestant.

I made the Pope head of the church again and put the stained glass, wall paintings and statues back into the churches.

I was very popular when I first became queen soon after Edward died.

I was 37 and I was the first woman to rule England on her own.

In 1554 I had to put down a rebellion that wanted to make my Protestant sister Elizabeth queen.

I believed that priests were people with special powers and should not marry like ordinary people.

My marriage to Philip II of Spain made me unpopular. Many English people did not want a Catholic foreigner as king. They were afraid he would control England.

I became quite ill, and very depressed. My half-sister Elizabeth became queen after me. She was a Protestant.

I had to burn 300 people at the stake because they refused to become Catholics. Most of them were ordinary working people. People blame me! I believe I was given the nickname 'Bloody Mary'.

ACTIVITIES

1. Make a list of all the differences you can find between Edward's and Mary's Church. Use the text and pictures to help with your answer.
2. Which of Edward's problems resulted from him being a minor?
3. Which of Mary's problems resulted from her being a woman?
4. In what ways were the problems they faced different?

1533	1540		1550		1560		1570

1533	1558	1559	1563	1568
Elizabeth is born	Elizabeth becomes Queen	The Elizabethan religious settlement	The first Elizabethan Poor Law is passed	Mary, Queen of Scots flees to England and is imprisoned

1558 – 1603

Gloriana: the queen of indecision?

At Tilbury Docks

In the summer of 1588 the Spanish Armada set out. 122 ships carrying 17,000 men sailed up the English Channel. They were on their way to join forces with the Spanish army in the Netherlands, led by the Duke of Parma. The Armada, with the army on board, would then attack England.

With an invasion expected at any moment, Elizabeth decided to go to Tilbury where her army had gathered. Her councillors were fearful for her safety and pleaded with her not to go, but she was determined.

On 8 August the Queen appeared before her troops dressed in a white velvet gown with a shining silver breastplate. Before her walked a page carrying her silver helmet on a white cushion. As drummers and pipers played, the Queen inspected her troops.

The following morning Elizabeth returned to the camp. She was greeted with a burst of applause so loud that 'the earth and air did sound like thunder', as though she was 'in the midst and heat of battle'. Then, 'most bravely mounted on a most stately steed', she spoke to her troops.

SOURCE A

Elizabeth appearing before her troops at Tilbury Docks

'My loving people,' she cried, 'I know I have the body of a weak and feeble woman, but I have the heart and stomach of a King, and a King of England too, and think foul scorn that Parma or Spain, or any Prince of Europe, should dare to invade the borders of my realm.'

Soon after delivering this speech Elizabeth was told that Parma was due to set sail. She was urged to return to London for safety, but she refused. She would fight and die with her people. But as night fell, the danger had passed...

	1580		1590		1600 1603		
1569	1572	1580's	1587	1588	1601	1603
The Northern Rebellion	The first compulsory local Poor Law tax is passed	Treatment of Catholics becomes harsher	Mary, Queen of Scots is executed	The Spanish Armada is defeated	The Elizabethan Poor Law is passed	Elizabeth dies

ACTIVITIES

1. Why do you think Elizabeth was advised not to go to Tilbury to see her troops?
2. Look at the story of the Armada. What impression does it give you of Elizabeth?
3. Look at Sources A and B. How do you think Elizabeth wanted people to see her?

The Elizabethan Golden Age: image or reality?

Elizabeth became queen on the death of her half-sister, Mary, in 1558. She was just 25 years old.

Mary's death had been greeted with joy by Londoners. Much was expected of the new queen. Huge crowds turned out when she arrived in London and there were ten days of feasting and dancing after her coronation. Even the weather seemed better than it had been during Mary's reign.

> 'It pleased God to send a calm quiet season, a clear and lovely sunshine and a world of blessings by Queen Elizabeth.'

From Chronicles of England, Scotland and Ireland *by Ralph Holinshed, 1587*

The reign of Elizabeth I is often regarded as a Golden Age in English history. Gloriana, the Faerie Queene, ruled her people with love, and they responded with unfailing loyalty, service and devotion. During her 45 years on the throne, Englishmen sailed the world, explored previously unknown lands and defeated enemies with acts of great courage and heroism. An image was created of Elizabeth as a powerful monarch who inspired her people.

> But how close is the image to the reality of Elizabeth as queen? Was she really a strong and powerful monarch who reigned over a golden age of achievements? Or was this just a myth created by Elizabeth and her councillors? Let's examine the problems she faced and how she dealt with them to help us decide...

SOURCE B

The 'Rainbow' portrait of Elizabeth, painted in about 1600

33

What problems did Elizabeth face in 1558?

In 1558 England was in 'a sad state', according to the new queen. To many it seemed that Elizabeth would be unable to overcome the problems she faced. It was not even certain that she would remain queen long enough to begin tackling them.

Elizabeth's claim to the throne was disputed. She was the daughter of Henry VIII and Anne Boleyn. But Anne had been found guilty of adultery and treason. Her marriage to the king had been dissolved and she had been executed. As a result Elizabeth had been declared illegitimate, which meant she did not have a claim to the throne. Although Henry had named her in his will as his successor after Edward and Mary, she was never declared legitimate.

She was also a woman. Mary had been England's first female monarch and it had not been a happy experience. At that time women were seen as weak and unfit to hold power in a male-dominated world.

There were also difficult decisions to make...

Foreign policy

England was just a minor power on the edge of Europe. Spain and France were the major European powers. Both could be serious threats to Elizabeth's England. In 1558 England and Spain were allies against France, but King Philip of Spain was the leader of the Counter-Reformation in Europe. If Elizabeth made England a Protestant country again he could become a very dangerous enemy. King Henry II of France had troops in Scotland, whose rulers were his allies. England lacked weapons, and her defences and fortresses were in a state of ruin. What could Elizabeth do?

Religion

After a quarter of a century of Reformation and Counter-Reformation, the people of England were divided by deep religious differences. It is not certain how many people were Catholics or Protestants in 1558. It is likely that there were more Protestants in the towns than in the countryside and in the South-East rather than in the North and West of the country. What would Elizabeth do?

Finance

In 1558 the government was £266,000 in debt – an enormous sum of money in those days. The main reason for this was Queen Mary's support for her husband King Philip of Spain's foreign wars. How could Elizabeth raise more money?

Marriage and succession

Everyone expected that Elizabeth would marry quickly and produce an heir to continue the Tudor dynasty. That was, after all, the duty of a royal princess. But the people did not want a foreign prince ruling England, and if she married an Englishman she risked giving too much power to one family. What should she do?

Mary, Queen of Scots

Mary, Queen of Scots was Elizabeth's cousin and heir. She was also a Catholic, half-French and had a rival claim to the English throne. She grew up in the French court and became Queen of France when she married Francis II. She could easily become the focus of Catholic opposition to Elizabeth. How should Elizabeth deal with her?

The poor

In the sixteenth century the population of England grew rapidly, from three to four million people. At the same time there was less work for ordinary people to do on the land. This was because landowners were fencing off the common land and keeping sheep rather than growing crops. There was more money to be made in selling wool and cloth than in growing food. Prices were also rising faster than wages. The result was that there were many more poor people in England. Henry VIII had dissolved the monasteries that had given relief to the poor, and the Treasury was empty! What could Elizabeth do?

ACTIVITIES

1. Which of the problems that Elizabeth faced in 1558 do you think needed dealing with most urgently?

2. Which of these problems do you think was the most difficult to solve? Why?

Finding out about Elizabeth

At the end of this unit you are going to be putting together a new exhibition on Elizabeth for Hatfield House.

At the age of just three months old, Princess Elizabeth was given her own home at Hatfield. She was here when her mother was executed and she was declared illegitimate. And it was in the park at Hatfield on the morning of 17 November 1558, as she sat reading a book in the bitter cold under an old oak tree, that she was approached by the lords of the realm, who knelt before her and saluted her as their queen. Elizabeth, it is said, sank to her knees on the grass and in Latin pronounced 'This is the Lord's doing: it is marvellous in our eyes.' She then rose to her feet, led the way back to the palace, and got on with the business of ruling England.

Historians have interpreted Elizabeth's reign in many different ways. Here are some of the issues about which they disagree:

- **How decisive she was.** Did she take decisive action, or did she avoid making decisions? If she avoided making decisions, was this because she couldn't make up her mind, or because she judged that the problem would just go away?

- **How successful she was.** Did she solve problems effectively, or did she create more problems for the future?

- **How strong and powerful she was.** Did she inspire her people, or was this just an image created by her advisers?

Your exhibition will show your own interpretation of Elizabeth as queen. You will need to think about the issues above as you work through the rest of the unit.

The problem of religion

When Elizabeth became queen in 1558 people were tired of the religious quarrels of Edward and Mary's reigns and desperately wanted the issue of religion to be settled.

Although Elizabeth was religious she did not like the extreme views of some Catholics and Protestants. 'There is,' she said, 'only one Jesus Christ and all the rest is a dispute over trifles.' So Elizabeth's religious settlement tried to find a middle ground that would please most of her people.

In 1559, in the Act of Supremacy, Parliament supported her in creating the Church of England, with Elizabeth as its **Supreme Governor**. In the Act of Uniformity, passed at the same time, church services were changed from Latin to English and the Prayer Book was adapted to allow Catholics and Protestants to use it. The churches were not stripped of all of their decorations as they had been in Edward's reign, but people could be fined if they did not attend services. Most people were happy with the middle way of the new Church of England.

SOURCE A

'Even those who were Catholics before did not notice any great difference in the religion set up by Elizabeth save only the change in language.'

Father Baker, a Catholic writing at the time

Some people, however, were not. Catholics with strong beliefs held services at home rather than attend church. Extreme Protestants, known as Puritans, also disapproved of the changes. They thought the reforms had not gone far enough! In 1569 there was a revolt by Catholics in the north, known as the Northern Rebellion. This was quickly put down and over 700 were executed. Within a few months the Pope excommunicated Elizabeth.

Elizabeth was now open to plots from Catholics for the rest of her reign.

SOURCE B

'We do declare her to be deprived of her title to the Kingdom. Also the nobility, subjects and people of the Kingdom to be forever **absolved** from all duty and obedience to her.'

Bull of Excommunication, Pope Pius V, 1570

Elizabeth's religious settlement became increasingly strained. From the 1580s onwards **Jesuit** priests began to arrive in England to support Catholics and encourage them to stay loyal to the Pope. At the same time the threat of an invasion by Catholic Spain grew. As a result the treatment of Catholics became harsher. Fines for not attending church increased from a **shilling** a week to £20 a month. Catholic priests were open to execution for treason, and more than 100 priests were arrested and killed. A number of Jesuit priests escaped the **gallows** by hiding in **priest holes**.

A Puritan family at home

The Priest's Hole

A priest hole at Coughton Court

Absolved
free from blame

Gallows
where people were hanged

Jesuit
a special missionary order of Catholic priests

Priest holes
very small secret rooms, built in a number of Elizabethan great houses owned by Catholics

Shilling
small silver coin in old currency (equivalent to modern 5p)

Supreme Governor
person with overall control of the Church of England

ACTIVITIES

1. Read Source A. Do you think most Catholics were happy with Elizabeth's religious changes?

2. When during Elizabeth's reign do you think Source A might have been written? Why?

3. Do you think the Pope's Bull (Source B) would have made all Catholics turn against Elizabeth?

4. Do you think Elizabeth acted decisively or indecisively over the problem of religion?

5. Do you think Elizabeth dealt successfully with the problem of religion? Why do you think this?

Finding out about Elizabeth

You are now going to produce your first panel for the exhibition on Elizabeth at Hatfield House. It should include:

- a heading: Elizabeth and religion
- three text boxes
  - the problem
  - what she did
  - your judgement of her actions
- two relevant images.

Remember, you can also do your own research. You do not have to rely on the information here! You can decide how to present your work – it might be a PowerPoint presentation, a poster, or a page in your exercise book.

The problem of **marriage and the succession**

In 1559 Elizabeth stood before her Parliament. She told them:

SOURCE A

'This shall be for me sufficient that a marble stone shall declare that a Queen, having reigned such a time, lived and died a virgin.'

A few years later, in 1566, Elizabeth again faced her Parliament. This time, she promised them she would marry.

SOURCE B

'I say again, I will marry as soon as I can, and I hope to have children, otherwise I would never marry.'

And yet, in the same year, she also said the following.

SOURCE C

'I will have but one mistress and no master.'

Confused? Her councillors certainly were. Elizabeth's refusal to decide one way or the other about marrying drove many of them to despair. Just what was going on?

Choices, choices...

As queen of England, Elizabeth was the most **eligible** woman in Europe, and she was certainly not short of suitors!

The problem was, no one seemed to be quite right. Perhaps it would be better not to marry at all? On the other hand, a marriage could provide an important alliance for England. Most importantly, if she did not marry, she would have no children to succeed her. Mary, Queen of Scots was Elizabeth's nearest relative, and Mary was a Catholic.

Philip II

Job: King of Spain

Religion: Catholic (very devout)

Previous relationships: Widower; previously married to Mary Tudor.

Good points: very rich and powerful. Spain would be a strong foreign ally.

Bad points: Leader of the Counter-Reformation, and persecutor of Protestants. He was unpopular in England as Mary had spent a lot of money to pay for his wars.

Archduke Charles

Job: Ruler of Austria

Religion: Catholic

Good points: Catholics would welcome the marriage. He would bring an alliance with the powerful Habsburg family.

Bad points: Protestants would not like the marriage, causing religious divisions. Elizabeth was not keen on him.

Eric of Sweden

Job: King of Sweden

Religion: Protestant

Good points: He was a Protestant, in love with Elizabeth, and popular in England.

Bad points: He was not rich, and Sweden would not be a strong ally in Europe.

Elizabeth continued marriage negotiations into the 1580s. In the end, though, she never married. She said she would remain a 'virgin queen', married to her people.

Francis, Duke of Anjou

Job: Brother of the King of France

Religion: Catholic

Good points: An alliance with France would help protect England against Spain. Elizabeth affectionately called him her Frog.

Bad points: He was Catholic and many English people disliked the French. He was not good looking and was scarred from the small pox.

Robert Dudley, Earl of Leicester

Job: English nobleman

Religion: Protestant

Good points: Attractive and witty. Elizabeth was rumoured to be in love with him.

Bad points: He was already married! There were rumours Elizabeth and Dudley were having an affair. Marrying him would damage her reputation. He was very ambitious and might use the marriage to advance his family. The marriage would not give England a foreign ally.

Robert Devereux, Earl of Essex

Job: English nobleman

Religion: Protestant

Good points: Young and good looking. Elizabeth's favourite when she was in her fifties.

Bad points: Arrogant, ambitious and reckless. He tried to lead a coup, which failed. In 1601 Elizabeth reluctantly had him executed.

ACTIVITIES

1. This is a list of reasons why Elizabeth did not marry. Pick the one that you think is most likely to be true. Explain your choice.
   - She did not want to upset her people.
   - She did not want to upset her ministers.
   - She did not want to upset her nobles.
   - To keep England safe from attack.
   - To keep power for herself.
   - She couldn't decide who to marry.

2. Could Elizabeth have had different reasons for not marrying a Catholic, Protestant, foreigner or noble?

3. Do you think Elizabeth really wanted to marry? Or did she say she would marry only to please her people?

4. What impression do you now have of Elizabeth?

NEW WORDS

Eligible
rich, attractive and not married

Finding out about Elizabeth

You are now going to produce your second panel for the exhibition on Elizabeth at Hatfield House. It should include:

- a heading: Elizabeth: Marriage and succession
- three text boxes:
  - the problem
  - what she did
  - your judgement of her actions
- two relevant images.

Remember, you can also do your own research!

The problem of Mary Queen of Scots

Mary, Queen of Scots was Elizabeth's Catholic cousin and heir, and the prize of the English throne was always on her mind. What's more, many people in Europe thought she had a stronger claim than Elizabeth herself...

On the death of Mary's first husband, the French **Dauphin**, in 1561, she returned to Scotland. Elizabeth's arch-rival was now living right on her doorstep. To make matters worse, Mary married Lord Darnley, who also had a strong claim to the English throne. However, Darnley was not popular in Scotland and was murdered in mysterious circumstances. Just three months after his death, Mary married his suspected assassin, James Bothwell. Almost at once the Scots revolted against Mary and she was captured. She was forced to give up the throne and her son James became King of Scotland.

Mary escaped and fled to England in 1568. As many people had feared, she quickly became the focus of Catholic plots against Elizabeth. Already, in 1569, she was at the centre of the Northern Rebellion. Elizabeth's advisers urged her to take decisive action against Mary. Yet Elizabeth refused to act against her cousin. The plots continued for nearly 20 years.

Elizabeth had good reason to be wary of doing anything drastic. Mary was a fellow queen, and had strong support in Europe. Then finally, in 1586, Mary's luck ran out. Elizabeth's spies discovered that Mary had been secretly corresponding with a Catholic plotter, Anthony Babington. Babington was arrested, tortured and executed. Mary was put on trial and found guilty of treason.

Mary, Queen of Scots

SOURCE A

'For the dispatch [murder] of the usurper [Elizabeth] there be six noble gentlemen, all my private friends, who for the love they bear to the Catholic cause and your Majesty's service will undertake that execution.'

Babington's letter to Mary, Queen of Scots

SOURCE B

'Everything being prepared, and the forces being ready, I must in some way be got from here to await foreign help.'

Part of Mary's letter to Babington, used as evidence against her at her trial

ACTIVITIES

1. Does Babington's letter (Source A) prove that Mary wanted Elizabeth killed? Explain your answer.

2. Does Source B prove that Mary approved of the plot and was guilty? Explain your answer.

The Babington plotters

The execution of Mary, Queen of Scots

Elizabeth's councillors urged her to execute Mary. Still she delayed. It was not until the following year that she signed Mary's death warrant. Even then, she changed her mind, and the Council had the sentence carried out without her permission. On 8 February, 1587, Mary was executed. When Elizabeth heard the news she flew into a rage, but it was too late.

ACTIVITIES

1. What advantages were there in delaying making a decision about what to do with Mary?

2. What disadvantages were there in delaying?

3. Why do you think Elizabeth was so reluctant to execute Mary?

4. What impression do you now have of Elizabeth as queen?

NEW WORDS

Dauphin
the heir to the French throne

Finding out about Elizabeth

You are now going to produce your third panel for the exhibition on Elizabeth at Hatfield House. It should include:

- a heading: Elizabeth and Mary, Queen of Scots

- three text boxes:
  - the problem
  - what she did
  - your judgement of her actions

- two relevant images.

Remember, you can also do your own research!

The problem of
relations with other countries

As Elizabeth had feared, Mary's execution caused uproar in Europe. One year later Elizabeth stood on Tilbury docks, trying to rally her troops as the Spanish Armada sailed towards England. Things might have looked bleak for England in 1588 but the fact remained that Elizabeth had successfully kept the country out of war for 30 years. Given the odds she faced, this was remarkable. How had she done it?

Avoiding war

When Elizabeth became queen, the situation did not look promising.

SOURCE A

'The Queen poor, the realm exhausted... divisions amongst ourselves; wars with France and Scotland; the French king bestriding the realm, having one foot in Calais and the other in Scotland.'

An official at the English court describing the situation in 1558

Elizabeth knew that at all costs, she must avoid war. One way that Elizabeth dealt with foreign relations was to keep everyone guessing about whom she would marry. She also encouraged both Catholic and Protestant suitors. Elizabeth realised that marriage negotiations were almost as effective as marriages in making alliances. They could also be ended when no longer convenient! This helped England to stay safe from attack for some time. But this did not always work. Philip of Spain never forgave her for refusing to marry him.

Another tactic was to help Protestant rebels in Catholic countries. Open assistance would have provoked war. Instead, by secretly supporting rebels in Scotland, France and the Netherlands, Elizabeth hoped that her enemies would be too busy fighting their own people to bother with England. For a while, it seemed to work.

The biggest problem was Spain. Since the 1560s and 1570s, Spain had been fighting

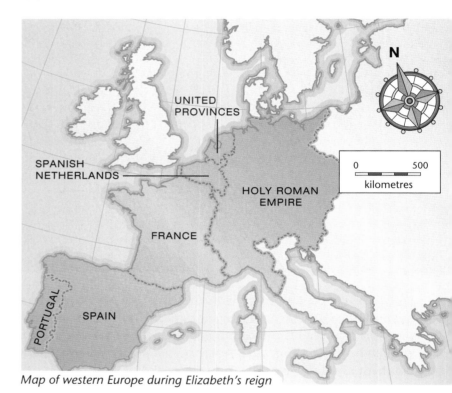

Map of western Europe during Elizabeth's reign

Protestant rebels in the Netherlands, where Philip II was also king. Elizabeth knew that if Philip ever managed to beat the rebels, his next target would be England. Many on her Council urged her to send military aid, but Elizabeth refused to commit herself. It wasn't until 1585, when war against Spain seemed inevitable anyway, that she finally sent English troops to fight on the side of the Dutch.

Eventually Elizabeth's actions proved too much for Phillip. She had aided the Dutch rebels, allowed English pirates to attack Spanish treasure ships and had executed Mary, a fellow queen. He began to plan an invasion of England.

ACTIVITIES

Spain attacked England just one year after Mary's execution. Does this change your view of Elizabeth's actions towards Mary? Explain your answer.

The Spanish Armada

The Spanish Armada

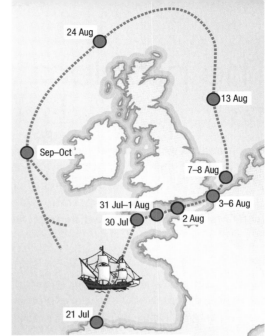
The route of the Spanish Armada

In May 1588 the 122 ships of the Spanish Armada set sail. On board were 8,000 sailors and 17,000 soldiers. In late July they were sighted off the coast of Cornwall. Beacons were lit along the coast, spreading the news.

But the Armada, instead of attacking, anchored off Calais. On 28 July, at dead of night, blazing fireships were carried on the tide into the closely packed Spanish fleet. The Spanish, afraid that their wooden boats would catch fire, scattered. The following day, the English fleet attacked at Gravelines. Neither side won the battle and the Spanish commander decided to head northwards. It was a fateful decision. With English ships chasing them, the Spanish fleet sailed towards the dangerous North Sea. The only way back to Spain was around the top of Scotland and Ireland. Terrible gales destroyed many ships. Only 67 ships and 10,000 men made it back to Spain. Against the odds, the Armada had been defeated.

However, England remained under threat from a further Spanish attack for the rest of Elizabeth's reign.

SOURCE B

'Many of our largest ships are still missing, and on the ships that are here there are many sick. Your Majesty, believe me when I assure you that we are very weak. How do you think we can attack so great a country as England with such a force as ours is now?'

The commander of the Spanish Armada, writing to Philip II after he returned to Spain following the defeat of the Armada

ACTIVITIES

1. On which occasions was Elizabeth decisive in her relations with other countries?

2. Over which issues did she avoid taking definite decisions?

3. Why did she sometimes avoid taking decisive action?

4. What impression do you now have of Elizabeth as queen?

Finding out about Elizabeth

You are now going to produce your fourth panel for the exhibition on Elizabeth at Hatfield House. It should include:

- a heading: Elizabeth and relations with other countries

- three text boxes:
  - the problem
  - what she did
  - your judgement of her actions

- two relevant images.

Remember, you can also do your own research!

The problem of **how to get money**

Taxes, trade and trafficking...

Every monarch worried about money. For the first half of her reign, Elizabeth managed to get by, mostly by raising taxes. The Queen also encouraged, and invested in, trade, which grew more important and profitable during her reign. She supported trading companies like the East India Company.

She also supported adventurers like Sir Francis Drake as they travelled the world in search of undiscovered lands and treasure. Many of these explorers were also **privateers**. Drake in particular enraged the Spanish by repeatedly raiding their settlements in South America and capturing their treasure ships. Far from stopping him, Elizabeth knighted him when he returned from his round-the-world voyage in 1580. She also helped finance a voyage by John Hawkins to West Africa to buy slaves to sell to the Spanish in South America. Despite the damage piracy did to relations with Spain, Elizabeth had a strong motive to turn a blind eye – she often received a share of the gold from captured Spanish treasure ships.

SOURCE A

Sir Francis Drake

SOURCE B

Sir Francis Drake's ship, The Golden Hind, attacking a Spanish treasure ship

Drake being knighted by Elizabeth. A nineteenth-century painting

Monopolies

But after the defeat of the Armada, the war with Spain, which continued until Elizabeth's death, and a rebellion in Ireland put huge strain on England's finances. Treasure and taxes were no longer enough. Elizabeth was forced to sell royal land. She also sold monopolies. Someone with a monopoly had the sole right to trade in a particular type of product. They could charge what they wished. Unfortunately this system tended to drive up prices. The price of salt increased eleven-fold! Elizabeth found herself in a fight with Parliament in 1597. She promised to look into the problem. By 1601 nothing had been done and Elizabeth again faced angry MPs. She promised to take action, but monopolies remained a problem for her successors, James I and Charles I. Even with the extra income, Elizabeth died leaving the government in debt to the tune of over £300,000.

SOURCE D

'Sir Wroth reported that monopolies were in force for currants, iron, cards, horns, ox shinbones, ashes, bottles, glasses, shreds of gloves, vinegar, sea coal, steel, brushes, pots, salt, lead, oil, transportation of leather, dried pilchards in the smoke, and divers [many] others. Upon reading of the patents, Mr Hackwell asked, "Is not bread there? Bread will be there, before the next parliament".'

From Tudor Economic Documents, R.H. Tawney and E. Power (eds.), 1924

ACTIVITIES

1. List the different ways in which Elizabeth tried to raise money.

2. In Source D, what does Mr Hackwell mean when he says, 'Is not bread there? Bread will be there before the next parliament'?

3. Which methods of raising money would have been most unpopular with:
   a) rich people
   b) poor people?

4. How successfully do you think Elizabeth dealt with the problem of raising money?

5. What impression do you now have of Elizabeth as queen?

NEW WORDS

Privateers
people who robbed ships

Finding out about Elizabeth

You are now going to produce your fifth panel for the exhibition on Elizabeth at Hatfield House. It should include:

- a heading: Elizabeth and raising money
- three text boxes:
  – the problem
  – what she did
  – your judgement of her actions
- two relevant images.

Remember, you can also do your own research!

The problem of
how to deal with the poor

Elizabeth's struggles to raise money were made worse by the growing problem of the poor. The monasteries used to help poor people, but Henry VIII had dissolved them. Although rich people often left money in their wills for the poor, there was never enough. There were more people. There were fewer jobs. Prices were rising faster than wages, and monopolies on many basic goods hit poor people the hardest. To make matters worse, there was a series of very bad harvests in the 1580s and 1590s. All this helped to increase the number of poor people, and the Treasury was nearly empty.

The Elizabethan Poor Laws

Elizabeth, like the other Tudor monarchs, passed laws to try and deal with the problem of the poor. In 1563, the Poor Law was passed. For the first time the poor were put into three different groups:

Those who wanted to work but could not were called the 'able-bodied, deserving poor'. They were to be given help.

In 1572 the first compulsory local Poor Law tax was introduced. This made helping the poor a local responsibility. In 1601 the Elizabethan Poor Law was passed. This put all the previous laws together. Overseers of the Poor were appointed in each parish, and the idle poor were taken to the poor-house and set to work. This law remained in place, with few changes, for over 200 years.

Those who were too young, too old or too ill to work were the 'impotent, deserving poor'. They were looked after in orphanages, hospitals or poor-houses.

Those who could work, but would not, were the 'idle poor'. They were known as vagrants. They could be punished. They were whipped through the streets until they learned to support themselves. Sometimes a letter V was branded on them with a hot iron.

'Hark, hark the dogs do bark,
The beggars are coming to town;
Some in rags and some in tags,
And one in a velvet gown.'

A popular nursery rhyme

ACTIVITIES

1. Pick out the lines in the nursery rhyme (Source A) that suggest:
   - There were different kinds of beggars
   - The beggars travelled in groups
   - The beggars were unpopular

2. The 1563 Poor Law was a big step forward. Can you suggest why another Poor Law was needed in 1601?

3. How successful was Elizabeth in dealing with the problem of the poor?

4. What impression do you now have of Elizabeth as queen?

Finding out about Elizabeth

You are now going to produce your sixth panel for the exhibition on Elizabeth at Hatfield House. It should include:

- a heading: Elizabeth and the problem of how to deal with the poor
- three text boxes:
  - the problem
  - what she did
  - your judgement of her actions
- two relevant images.

Making your mind up

So what do you really think of Elizabeth as a monarch? This is what Pope Sixtus V wrote about her. Remember – he was an enemy of Elizabeth's.

'She is a great Queen and were she only a Catholic she would be our dearly beloved. Just look at how well she governs! She is only a woman and yet she makes herself feared by Spain, by France, by all.'

At the beginning of the unit you were given three key issues about Elizabeth to consider. These were:

- **How decisive she was.** Did she take decisive action, or did she avoid making decisions? If she avoided making decisions, was this because she couldn't make up her mind, or because she judged that the problem would just go away?

- **How successful she was.** Did she solve problems effectively, or did she create more problems for the future?

- **How strong and powerful she was.** Did she inspire her people, or was this just an image created by her advisers?

You are now going to produce the final panel of your exhibition for Hatfield House in which you will answer these questions. It should include:

- a heading: choose a heading that sums up your impression of Elizabeth
- four text boxes:
  - how decisive she was
  - how successful she was
  - how strong and powerful she was
  - whether the image was stronger than the reality
- one image that sums up your impression of Elizabeth.

Remember, you can also do your own research!

Interpretations of history

What does Susan Brigden's book tell us about the Tudors... and about Susan Brigden?

Susan Brigden is Reader in Modern History at Lincoln College, Oxford. In her book *New Worlds, Lost Worlds: The Rule of the Tudors 1485–1603*, she gives us her **interpretation** of Tudor times.

The extract that follows is an edited version of her summary of the period. As you read it, remember that Elizabeth I, the last of the Tudors, was succeeded by James I, the first of the Stuarts. He was the son of the Catholic, Mary, Queen of Scots...

'Catholics expected a return to their faith. "We shall have a new world shortly," promised Babington. Yet Protestantism slowly gained the victory, and a world was lost that could not be restored.

The supporters of Protestantism had changed religion and society, but at great cost. There was physical destruction: the altars and shrines of the parish churches were torn down; monasteries lay in ruins or were converted into mansions for the gentry.

Even more traumatic was the loss of Catholic beliefs. The world of shared faith was broken, and the Christian community was divided.

At the Reformation Christians were forced to choose between two churches. Each one claimed to be the true Church. Most people did their public duty by **conforming** through all the Tudor reformations and obeyed the royal will. Some still clung to their old faith in private. The need to support a family and earn a living gave them little choice. For most, life was a struggle.

Nevertheless, no one was untouched by the great transformations which Reformation brought. As Elizabeth's reign drew to its natural close, there were reasons for unease...'

All historians bring their own experiences, interests and ideas to their study of history. Some are more interested in political history (kings, queens and governments), some in social history (everyday life). Others prefer economic history (to do with money) or religious history. This is why historians' interpretations of the past differ so much.

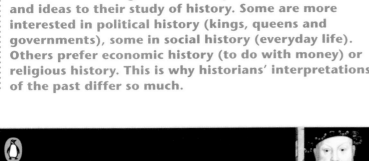

'Gets into the mind and under the skin of Tudor England'
David Starkey

NEW WORLDS, LOST WORLDS

The Rule of the Tudors 1485–1603

SUSAN BRIGDEN

ACTIVITIES

1. What kind of history do you think Susan Brigden is most interested in? How can you tell?

2. What changes does she think the Reformation had brought to Tudor England? Does she think they were good changes, or bad? Choose some words or phrases she uses to support your answer.

3. Do you think Susan Brigden thinks the Tudors were good rulers of England, or not? What words or phrases does she use to get her opinion across to her readers?

4. Does Susan Brigden's interpretation of Tudor times reflect what you have read in this book? Does she agree with our view? Or does she disagree? How can you explain any differences between us?

NEW WORDS

Conforming
accepting the current rules
Interpretation
view

Reconstructing history
Shakespeare's Globe

In 1600 most plays were performed in the courtyards of inns. But there were a number of theatres just outside the city of London. The largest were on the south bank of the River Thames and included the Rose, Swan and Globe.

The Globe theatre was owned by a group of actors. They each took a share of the profits. One of them was William Shakespeare. He wrote many of the plays that were performed at the Globe.

As many as 15,000 people a week attended plays in London. A theatre performed up to six different plays a week. They managed this with a cast of about 15 male actors, who played all the roles.

In 1613 the thatched roof of the Globe was set on fire during a performance of *Henry VIII*. No one was hurt, but one man's trousers caught light. He was saved when someone put out the flames with beer. The whole theatre was burnt down in less than two hours. A new theatre was built on the same spot. This time the roof was tiled. The Globe did well until the English Civil War in 1642 when Parliament closed down all theatres. Two years later the Globe was pulled down to clear space for new houses.

For the next 300 years the Globe was almost forgotten. Then, in 1949, the American actor Sam Wanamaker decided to visit the site of the theatre. He was dismayed to find that all there was to see was a plaque saying, 'Here stood Shakespeare's Globe.' He decided to do something

The south bank of the River Thames and the theatres in the early seventeenth century

about it. Slowly the idea grew to rebuild the Globe near to its original site, and to make it the most accurate reconstruction possible.

'All the world's a stage,
And all the men and women merely players:
They have their exits and their entrances;
And one man in his time plays many parts.'

From As You Like It, *Act 2, Scene 7,*
William Shakespeare, 1599

ACTIVITIES

1. Write down as many differences as you can between the original Globe and a typical modern theatre.

2. Why do you think all theatres were built outside the City of London?

3. Why do you think Sam Wanamaker was dismayed to find only a plaque marking the site of the Globe?

Why rebuild the Globe?

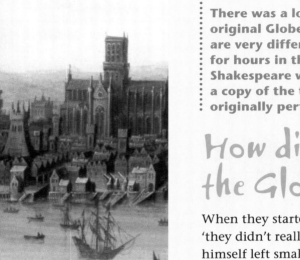

There was a lot of argument about the idea of building a copy of the original Globe. Some experts said there was no point. Audiences today are very different from those in 1600. Would they put up with standing for hours in the open to watch a play? Other experts said that, since Shakespeare wrote 12 of his best plays while at the Globe, building a copy of the theatre would help us understand how the plays were originally performed.

How did they know what the Globe looked like?

When they started the project to rebuild the Globe the answer to this question was 'they didn't really'. There were just a few pieces of evidence to go on. Shakespeare himself left small clues about the theatre in his plays.

> **'Can this cockpit hold**
> **The vasty fields of France? or even we cram**
> **Within this wooden O the very casques**
> **That did affright the air at Agincourt?'**

These lines are from the play *Henry V*. The 'wooden O' refers to the shape of the Globe theatre.

There are a few pictures dating from the seventeenth century which show the south bank of the Thames. These include views of the Globe and the other theatres, but could they be trusted to be accurate?

There were some points that nearly everyone agreed on. The Globe was made of wood. It was roughly round in shape. It had three stories, and there was an open yard in the middle.

There was evidence from other theatres. The building contract still exists for the Fortune theatre that was built to compete with the Globe. The document gives details of how the Fortune was to be built. This evidence, together with that from the pictures, made it possible to estimate the size of the original Globe.

We also have a drawing of the inside of the Swan theatre. This is a really important image because it is the only original picture we have of the inside of a theatre at that time.

deWitt sketch of the Swan theatre

What did the experts decide to build?

Throughout the 1980s various sketches, paintings and models were made, showing what the Globe theatre was like. Here is one artist's impression of how the Globe might have looked.

We now know that Paul Cox did not get his painting quite right. In January 1989 archaeologists found the remains of the nearby Rose theatre. From there they worked out where the Globe had originally stood. They managed to dig up part of the original stone and brick foundations. They discovered that the Globe did not have 24 sides, as Paul Cox painted it, but 20 sides. They also found it was 100 metres in diameter. That was larger than they had originally thought.

An aerial view of the Globe by Paul Cox

How did they build the new theatre?

In 1991 work started on the foundations of the new Globe. Two years later, building began. The theatre was put up just as in 1600, without glue or nails to join the wooden frame. Instead wooden pegs were used to hold the timbers together. For the first time since the Great Fire of 1666 a thatched roof was put on a London building. The reeds used were specially treated and a sprinkler system was placed in the thatch.

The outside of the new Globe

Have they made any changes since it was built?

The new Globe opened in 1997. Three seasons later a few changes were made. The bases of pillars were made smaller to make it easier to see the stage. Part of the balcony was made bigger which made some scenes easier to act. These changes were based on real experiences in using the theatre. That means the new Globe may now be more like the original than before.

Inside the new Globe today

So is the new Globe completely accurate?

A reconstruction can never be completely accurate. A certain amount of guesswork is inevitable. But the guesses made when building the Globe were always based on some kind of evidence. Sometimes clues had to come from art and old houses, rather than real theatres. However, some changes from the original were essential. Lighting was put into the new theatre so performances could continue into the evening. Glass was added to the open windows to keep out the noise of traffic on the river. The new Globe is not the same as the original, but it is probably close.

ACTIVITIES

1. Add to your list of differences between the original Globe and a typical modern theatre.

2. Which details of the new Globe do you think are most likely to be right? Use the pictures and the text to help with your answers.

3. Which details of the new Globe do you think are most likely to be wrong? Use the pictures and the text to help with your answers.

4. Do you think the effort involved in building the new Globe was justified? Give a reason for your answer.

5. Do you think we'll ever know what it really looked like? Does it matter? Give reasons for your answer.

1492	1558	1562	1576	1577
Christopher Columbus reaches the West Indies	Elizabeth becomes Queen	Mercator's map first published. Hawkins' first slave voyage	Martin Frobisher first sails for the North West passage	Francis Drake sets off on his round-the-world voyage

1492 – 1622

Making the world smaller

A 'foolish' venture?

June 1576 and Martin Frobisher sails into the unknown in search of the North West passage to Asia. He rounds the southern tip of Greenland, coasts up the shores of Labrador and enters an inlet above the entrance to Hudson Bay. There he lands and takes possession of the area in the name of Queen Elizabeth. He gathers some of the products of the region, including a heavy, dark stone, before returning to England in the autumn.

Frobisher gives the stone to a man. His wife, in a passion, throws a fragment of it into the fire. Her husband snatches it out and drops it into vinegar. It glistens like burnished gold. The result is gold-fever...

The English arriving in Greenland

May 1577 and Frobisher, now funded by the newly-formed Cathay Company, sets off again. He sails in a royal naval ship provided by Queen Elizabeth, and is accompanied by two other vessels. This time he is searching for gold.

A chart showing Frobisher's Straits, produced in the sixteenth century

1583	**1587**	**1607**	**1620**
Ralph Fitch sets off for India	Colony on Roanoke Island established	Colony at Jamestown established	Pilgrim Fathers arrive in America

They land at the same inlet, load the ships with as much of the black stone as they can carry (about 200 tons), and return to England.

Queen Elizabeth appoints a commission to determine the value of the cargo. Very little gold – if any – is found in the black stone. Yet the commission decides to send another expedition to the region. Frobisher is placed in command of a fleet of 15 ships.

May 1578 and Frobisher sets sail once more. Only half the ships reach their destination. They return to England laden with the dark stones (about 2,000 tons), and not a single particle of gold is found. They have brought back 'Fools' Gold': the Cathay Company goes bankrupt...

ACTIVITIES

1. Where did Frobisher hope to get to through a 'North West passage'?

2. Who had paid for the voyage?

3. Why, despite *not* finding gold, was a third expedition sent?

4. What does Frobisher's story tell us about the motives for exploration and discovery in Elizabethan England?

Sir Martin Frobisher

Finding out about exploration

During this period, big improvements were made in mapmaking, as people's knowledge of the world changed. At the end of this unit, you will produce your own map of exploration: a concept map to show what motivated Elizabethan exploration and discovery. You will need to decide:

- how important **political** motives were
- how important **economic** motives were
- how important **religious** motives were
- how important **cultural** motives were.

By drawing your concept map, you will also be able to see how different motives were linked to each other.

1. Re-read the story of Martin Frobisher's voyage. Why did he sail to North America? List as many reasons as you can.

2. For each reason, decide whether his motives were political, economic, religious, or cultural, or a mixture of these.

3. Copy out the concept map below. Remember to leave plenty of space, as you will need to add to the map as you work through the unit. For each reason for exploration you find, add it to your map, linking it with an arrow to the type of motivation you think it is. If you think it was a mixture of types, you can draw an arrow to more than one box. One example has been started for you.

Economic

Political

search for gold
e.g. Martin Frobisher's
voyages to North America
in 1577 and 1578.

Religious

Cultural

No other world but England?

For people in many parts of England in 1500 London was as remote a place as China or India. A visiting ambassador wrote that the English thought:

> 'that there are no other men than themselves and no other world but England'

But this attitude changed. The biggest differences between England in 1500 and England in 1750 were the result of world trade. The change began to take place during the reign of Queen Elizabeth. This was a great age of English exploration, and it eventually led to the **foundation** of the British Empire.

> **So why had this happened?**

Money, money, money...?

Since the Middle Ages English merchants had traded with European countries, but now they wanted spices from the Far East. Cinnamon and cloves could be used to flavour meat. This was a time when there were no refrigerators and most food had to be salted to preserve it. Spices were very expensive because they had to be transported over land. If English merchants could trade directly with India and China, where those spices came from, they could make big profits.

Spain and Portugal had also been trying to find new routes to the Far East since the late fifteenth century. Portuguese explorers had sailed around the southern tip of Africa and into the Indian Ocean, setting up a string of bases on their way.

Meanwhile, an explorer called Christopher Columbus was convinced that he could reach China by sailing westwards across the Atlantic. He persuaded the King and Queen of Spain to sponsor a voyage. Columbus never found a route westwards to the Far East. Instead, he landed on the islands that today we know as the West Indies. He had 'found' a new world.

By the middle of the sixteenth century the Spanish controlled most of the trade with Central and South America. England needed to find new routes to Asia that would not risk attack by their enemies. So, the reign of Queen Elizabeth became a great age of exploration and discovery.

> **But why did it all happen at this time?**

Profit One successful voyage could make you very rich indeed, and perhaps lead to honours and titles. Monarchs, rich merchants and bankers were keen to sponsor voyages.

NORTH AMERICA

Gold and silver Europe had few natural resources of precious metals. Gold and silver were in high demand. A lot had been found in central and south America.

Key
-------- Important trade routes in the sixteenth and seventeenth centuries

Empire Spain had a huge empire in South America, and it was making her very rich. England wanted the same.

ANTARC

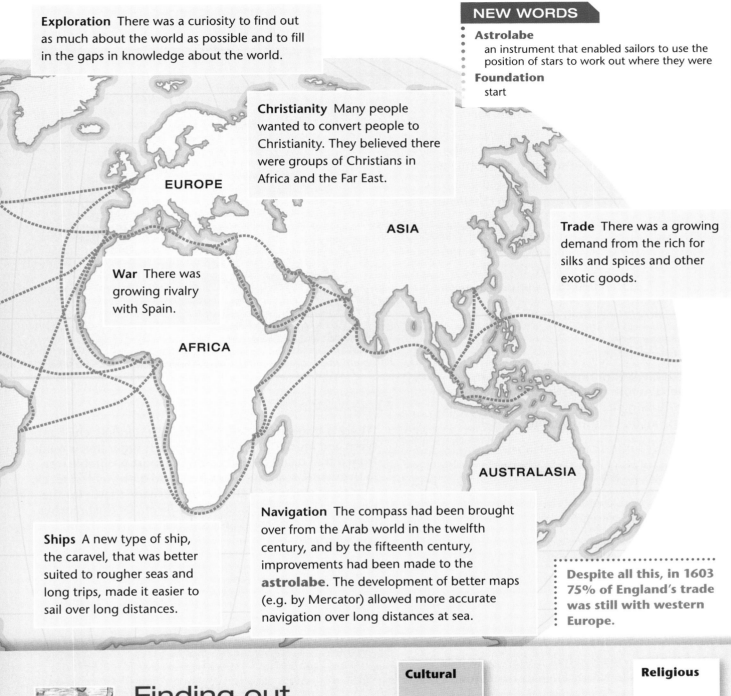

Exploration There was a curiosity to find out as much about the world as possible and to fill in the gaps in knowledge about the world.

Christianity Many people wanted to convert people to Christianity. They believed there were groups of Christians in Africa and the Far East.

EUROPE

ASIA

Trade There was a growing demand from the rich for silks and spices and other exotic goods.

War There was growing rivalry with Spain.

AFRICA

AUSTRALASIA

Ships A new type of ship, the caravel, that was better suited to rougher seas and long trips, made it easier to sail over long distances.

Navigation The compass had been brought over from the Arab world in the twelfth century, and by the fifteenth century, improvements had been made to the **astrolabe**. The development of better maps (e.g. by Mercator) allowed more accurate navigation over long distances at sea.

Despite all this, in 1603 75% of England's trade was still with western Europe.

Finding out about exploration

You now have a lot more explanations to add to your concept map! For each factor, decide whether it was a political, economic, religious or cultural motive, and add it to your map. If you think two motivations were linked, draw an arrow between them.

An example has been done for you:

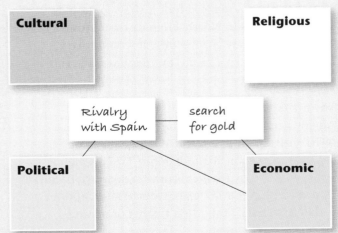

Cultural

Religious

Rivalry with Spain

search for gold

Political

Economic

Into the **unknown**
Over land to India

The story of Ralph Fitch gives an idea of what English explorers were prepared to face. Fitch travelled over land across the Syrian desert, through what is now Iraq, and eventually reached India. On the way he was twice imprisoned by the Portuguese (who thought he was a spy), but managed to escape. He then went on through Burma, Siam (Thailand) and down to the Malay coast. He got back to England in 1591 after a journey lasting eight years. Unfortunately, he was thought to be dead, so his possessions had been given away. Fitch wrote an account of his travels that was published in 1598.

Here are two extracts from his book:

SOURCE A

'By the River Euphrates is a strange thing to see: a mouth that doth continually throw forth boiling pitch with a filthy smoke. The Moors say that it is the mouth of Hell.'

Written about a place in what is now Iraq

ACTIVITIES

1. Can you work out what the 'boiling pitch' in Source A really was?

2. Why were descriptions written by explorers, like the one in Source B, useful to English merchants?

European merchants in India

SOURCE B

'There is trade in all sorts of spices, silk, sandals, elephants' teeth and much China work, and much sugar that is made from a tree called the palm. It is the most profitable tree in the world. It always bears fruit, and doth yield wine, oil, sugar and vinegar. Of the leaves are made thatch for the houses, sails for ships and mats to lie on. Of the branches they make their houses and brooms to sweep. Of the tree, wood for ships.'

Written about India

Colonising America

Some merchants realised that if they could help start new towns in North America the **colonists** would have to buy their goods. It would take a long time to make a profit, but regular trade was guaranteed.

The first attempts to settle the coast of North America ended in failure. The first settlement of 107 men organised by Sir Walter Raleigh on an island was soon abandoned. In 1587 Raleigh financed a colony further south on Roanoke Island. Two years later the 117 men, women and children had disappeared. Only their rusting or rotting possessions remained.

The English arriving in Virginia

The 1607 settlement at Jamestown in Chesapeake Bay was more successful. Despite disease that killed half of the 104 colonists and a war with local native Americans that nearly wiped the colonists out, the settlement survived. The settlers moved to better land away from the coast, built a new town and started growing tobacco with the help of African slaves.

A painting of the native American village of Pomeiooc, by John White. White sailed with Raleigh on one of his expeditions to America

A godly community

In December 1620 the crew of the *Mayflower* finally sighted land. They were sailing for Virginia, but in fact the land that they could see was Cape Cod. On board were 102 men, women and children. Many of them were Puritans. They were fleeing from James I, who had warned them,

> **"I will make them conform, or I will harry them out of the land, or else do worse."**

The group has become known as the 'Pilgrim Fathers'. The settlement they founded was called New Plymouth. But at first it seemed unlikely that the colony would survive. The pilgrims had arrived in the depths of winter, and by spring 51 of them had died of cold and disease. It was only when local native Americans showed them how to plant maize that they were able to grow enough food to survive. By October 1621, the colony was finally secure. To celebrate, a thanksgiving feast was held. From these early settlements the English spread to control almost the entire eastern coast of North America by 1750.

NEW WORDS

Colonists
settlers in a new country

ACTIVITIES

1. Roanoke became known as the Lost Colony. List some reasons why the colonists may have disappeared.

2. Why do you think that New Plymouth survived?

Finding out about exploration

1. Can you find any more reasons for exploration to add to your concept map?

Using your map:

2. Do you think all explorers were motivated by the same things?

3. Can you give examples of how different motives were linked to each other?

4. What do you think the most important reason for exploration in Elizabethan England was? Give some reasons for your answer.

| 1566 | 1570 | | 1580 | | 1590 | | 1600 | | 1610 | | 1620 | 1625 |

1566	1567	1587	1603	1604	1625
James born	James becomes king of Scotland	James's mother, Mary, Queen of Scots, is executed	James becomes James I of England	James writes 'A Counterblaste to Tobacco'	James dies

Link 4

'The wisest fool in Christendom'?

In March 1603 Queen Elizabeth I died. Immediately a messenger rode 650 kilometres north to Edinburgh to tell the King of Scotland. James VI of Scotland knew he was now also James I of England. He was the first of the Stuarts to rule England.

This poem by Rudyard Kipling was first published in *A School History of England* in 1911. It shows the attitude towards James I at that time.

> The child of Mary Queen of Scots,
> A shifty mother's **shiftless** son,
> Bred up among **intrigues** and plots,
> Learned in all things, wise in none.
> Ungainly, babbling, wasteful, weak,
> Shrewd, clever, cowardly, **pedantic**,
> The sight of steel would **blanch** his cheek,
> The smell of baccy drove him frantic.
> He was the author of his line—
> He wrote that witches should be burnt;
> He wrote that monarchs were divine,
> And left a son who proved they weren't!

From A School History of England
by C.R.L. Fletcher and Rudyard Kipling, 1911

James I, King of England 1603 – 1625

James I: born 1566 – died 1625

👁 **ACTIVITY**

James became known as the 'wisest fool in Christendom', but his character was more complex. Try to decide what kind of person he was. Match each of the comments about James below to the lines of the poem. One way to do this is to make a copy of the poem and then write the correct letter alongside each line.

A James believed he ruled by **Divine Right**.

B James was known as one of the most educated monarchs of his day. He could speak fluent French, Greek and Latin, wrote books and supported other writers, including Shakespeare. However, James did not get on well with Parliament and he spent far too much money.

C When James died in 1625 his son Charles became king. After a civil war against Parliament Charles was beheaded in 1649.

D James wrote a book called A Counterblaste to Tobacco (1604). In it he described the 'vile custom of tobacco taking' as 'loathsome to the eye, hateful to the nose, and dangerous to the lungs'.

E James suffered from arthritis, weak legs and other illnesses. He also had a large tongue and tended to dribble.

F Mary, Queen of Scots was involved in a number of plots. She may even have been involved in the murder of her second husband.

G James was terrified that someone would try to **assassinate** him. He sometimes wore a padded jacket so nobody could stab him. This was in a time when people still expected their monarch to be a military leader.

H James had an unhappy childhood. As he grew up he learned that murder and plots were part of life at the Scottish royal court.

K Perhaps as many as 1,000 people were tried and executed for witchcraft during James's reign.

L James was the son of Mary, Queen of Scots and great-grandson of Margaret Tudor.

I James was the first of the Stuart line of monarchs to rule England.

J English court official Sir Anthony Weldon said James was 'very crafty and cunning'. He managed to keep England out of the religious wars happening in Europe. He also managed to keep the Church of England united, despite opposition from Catholics and radical Protestants.

👁 **ACTIVITIES**

1 What impression of James I do you have from the poem?

2 Do you believe the description of James in the poem? Why?

3 How would you go about checking if it was correct?

NEW WORDS

Assassinate
kill a leader

Blanch
turn white

Divine Right
the belief that God gave a monarch the right to rule

Intrigues
plotting

Pedantic
putting learning above everything

Shiftless
lazy

1603	1604	April 1604	May 1604	26 Oct 1605
James VI of Scotland becomes James I of England	Harsh anti-Catholic laws are passed	A group of Catholics plot to blow up King James	The plotters rent a house next to Parliament	Lord Monteagle receives a letter about the plot

Gunpowder, treason ...and plot?

Friday 31 January 1606

Thousands of people lined the route between the Tower of London and Westminster. They watched as four men were dragged through the streets on wooden **hurdles**. The four men knew what was waiting for them. They had been sentenced to a traitor's death.

'The traitor is not worthy to tread upon the face of the earth. He is to be drawn backward at a horse's tail, lying so near the ground to be unfit to take the common air.'

In the yard by Westminster Hall the hangman was ready. His job was to make sure that the prisoners did not die quickly.

'The traitor shall be strangled, being hanged up by the neck between heaven and earth. Then he is to be cut down alive.'

SOURCE A

Close to the hangman's **gibbet** a fire was burning. Here men were waiting with butchers' knives and cleavers. Their job was to cut open the prisoners while they were still alive. Next they had to pull out the traitor's bowels and heart.

'The traitor's privy parts shall be cut off and burnt before his face. His bowels and inner parts shall be taken out and burnt.'

Not all the executions went exactly as planned. The first to die was Thomas Winter. He made a speech and prayed that the King would become a Catholic. Next was Ambrose Rookwood. He was left hanging a little longer because he had asked to be forgiven. Robert Keyes was third. He tried to end his life quickly by jumping from the ladder. Keyes was unlucky, the rope broke and he was still alive for the rest of the punishment. The last to die was Guy Fawkes. He had been tortured and needed help to climb up on to the gibbet. After praying he jumped from the ladder and broke his neck. He was already dead when the rest of the terrible sentence was carried out.

The four men executed that Friday were not the first traitors to die in 1606. Sir Everard Digby, Robert Winter, John Grant and Thomas Bates had been **hanged, drawn and quartered** the day before in St Paul's Churchyard. Others were executed in the months that followed. All were accused of **treason**. They were involved in a plot to blow up the King and Parliament.

ACTIVITIES

1. Source A is not completely accurate. Why? (Clue: Do some counting.)

2. If Source A is not accurate, can it still provide useful evidence about the executions?

3. Why do you think so many people watched these executions?

4. Why do you think the traitors were given such a harsh punishment?

NEW WORDS

Gibbet
gallows for hanging criminals

Hanged, drawn and quartered
the punishment for traitors

Hurdles
wooden frames covered in woven branches

Treason
attempting to kill the king or overthrow the government

The execution of the plotters. This print was made soon after the executions

The final task was to cut off the prisoners' heads and chop their bodies into quarters. The heads would be set up on London Bridge to 'become a prey for the fowls of the air'.

Catholic conspiracy or Cecil set-up?

Eight men were executed in January 1606 – this is about as far as definite facts go in the story of the Gunpowder Plot. Read the story that follows carefully. Try to work out which information is definitely true, which is probably true, and which might not be true.

In 1603 English Catholics were pleased to have a new king. They knew that James had a Catholic wife. He appointed some Catholics to important posts. He stopped fining Catholics for not going to Protestant church services. But this did not last. James was under pressure to continue to **persecute** Catholics. His chief minister, Robert Cecil, told him that they obeyed foreign rulers. James changed his mind and reintroduced the fines. Catholic priests were ordered to leave England. But worse was to come.

In April 1604 a bill was introduced into Parliament. If it became law it would ruin many Catholic families. They would not even be able to make wills or be fully protected by the law. They were to be treated as enemies.

A small group of Catholics decided to act. Their leader, Robert Catesby, had the idea of killing the King and starting a revolt. The plan was to blow up the King as he met Parliament. The King's daughter, Princess Elizabeth, would then be kidnapped and made queen. If the plan succeeded, all her chief advisers would be Catholics.

In May 1604 the plotters rented a small house next to the House of Lords. For weeks they worked to tunnel under Parliament but their efforts were useless. Seeping water and the stone foundations of the House of Lords halted all progress. During this time four more men joined the plot. They were all trusted relatives of the original plotters. Then, in March 1605, the plotters managed to rent a coal cellar underneath Parliament. Guy Fawkes smuggled 36 barrels of gunpowder into the cellar. He placed bars of iron on top and covered these with a layer of wood.

The plotters in a print made later by a Dutch artist

Robert Winter   Christopher Wright   John Wright   Thomas Percy   Guido Fawkes   Robert Catesby   Thomas Winter

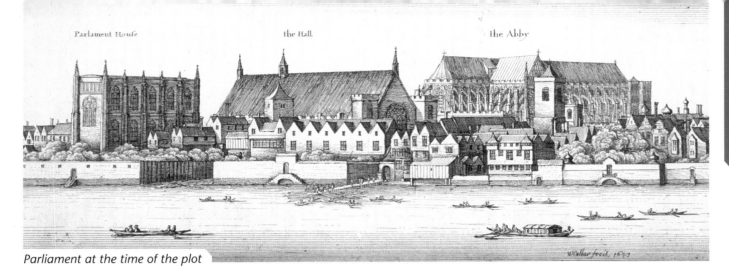

Parliament at the time of the plot

Outbreaks of plague in London delayed the meeting of Parliament. Some of the plotters left London, waiting for Parliament to meet on 5 November. Guy Fawkes, using the name John Johnson, was left in charge of the gunpowder.

The plotters knew there were Catholic lords who would be killed in the explosion if the plot went ahead. On 26 October the Catholic Lord Monteagle received an unsigned letter. The wording of the letter disturbed him enough to take it to Robert Cecil, one of the King's ministers. Cecil took the letter to the King. After reading it, James immediately guessed that there was a plan to blow him up.

On the night of 4 November Parliament was searched and Guy Fawkes was arrested. At first he insisted he was John Johnson, only a servant guarding his master's fuel. When he was searched, the tinder and slow matches he planned to use to start the explosion were found.

James ordered that Guy Fawkes be taken to the Tower of London and tortured. For two days he was stretched on the rack. At last, in agony, he confessed the names of all those involved in the plot.

The other plotters learned of Guy Fawkes' arrest. Those in London fled to the Midlands where they failed to find anyone who would help them. On 9 November 13 plotters were surrounded in Holbeach House in Staffordshire. They tried to break out but several were killed. The remaining plotters were soon captured and taken to London for questioning, trial and execution.

NEW WORDS

- **Persecute**
  pick on, or treat badly

Finding out about the plot

'Historians still argue over the events of 1605. Some believe it was a Catholic conspiracy. Others think Cecil knew about it and may even have been behind it from the start. At the end of this unit you will have to decide which theory you think is the most likely to be true.'

1. Make a copy of the table below, leaving enough space to add to it later. Decide which points from the story you think are important. How true do you think they are? Which theory do they support?

The Story of 1605	Catholic conspiracy?	Cecil set-up?
Definitely true	The plotters were Catholic. James had a Catholic wife	Cecil took the letter to the King
Probably true		
Might be true		

2. Which interpretation do you think is most likely to be true at the moment?

Who was **who**?

To understand the Gunpowder Plot it is important to know details about some of those involved. While reading about these five people think about information that might be significant in helping decide what happened and who was responsible.

The 'bomber'
Guy Fawkes

Guy Fawkes was born in York. Among his school friends were John and Christopher Wright. Both brothers later became involved in the plot.

Fawkes joined the Spanish army. He fought with them in France for nearly ten years. He was a strong and respected soldier. He was an expert with gunpowder.

In 1603 he visited Spain with other English Catholics. They tried to persuade the Spanish to invade England when Elizabeth died.

In 1604 Guy Fawkes was invited to England and sworn into the Gunpowder Plot.

NEW WORDS

Tower
  Tower of London – a royal castle often also used as a prison

The leader
Robert Catesby

Robert Catesby came from a Catholic family. When he was eight he saw his father arrested for the first time. The fines his family had to pay for not attending Protestant church services took a fifth of their income.

In 1593 Catesby married into a rich Protestant family. This money helped him finance the Gunpowder Plot.

Catesby sheltered Catholic priests who were in hiding from the government. He was arrested and sent to the **Tower** in 1596. In prison with him were John and Christopher Wright and Francis Tresham.

Catesby was involved in the Earl of Essex's rebellion in 1601. He was imprisoned and not released until he paid a heavy fine.

The chief minister
Robert Cecil

Robert Cecil was born with a slightly hunched back. His father was Lord Burghley, one of Elizabeth I's chief ministers. Burghley was involved in the execution of Mary, Queen of Scots.

In 1591 Queen Elizabeth made Cecil a member of the Privy Council. He went on to become Elizabeth's most important minister. Like his father, Cecil hated the Catholics.

Cecil was a clever politician and he had spies in England and Europe. He helped ensure the crown passed peacefully to James when Elizabeth I died. James rewarded Cecil for his support.

The government spy?
William Parker, Lord Monteagle

William Parker was a Catholic. He had close links with several of the plotters. He married Francis Tresham's sister.

He was captured in Essex's failed rebellion in 1601 but was released after paying a fine of £8,000.

Monteagle wrote to King James saying he had become a Protestant. Despite this he still had close links with Catholic friends and Thomas Winter (one of the plotters) was his secretary. In the summer of 1605 he met Robert Catesby and Francis Tresham. He told them he disliked King James.

After the plot was uncovered, Monteagle was treated as a hero. He was rewarded with land and £500 a year for life.

The plot traitor?
Francis Tresham

Tresham was probably the last man to join the Gunpowder Plot and when the plotters heard about the letter sent to Lord Monteagle they suspected Tresham. He managed to convince them that he was innocent. He also argued that the plot was discovered and that they should all flee.

On 2 November Tresham received a licence to travel abroad with 'two servants, three horses and 50 pounds in money'. He was the only plotter in London who did not flee after Fawkes was captured. Tresham was arrested on 12 November and taken to the Tower. He became ill and died in the Tower on 23 December. There were rumours that he had been poisoned.

Finding out about the plot

1. Using the information from this section, add to the table you began on page 65. Decide which details you think are important. How true do you think they are? Which theory do they support?

2. Which interpretation do you now think is most likely to be true? Look back at your anwer to activity 2 on page 65. Do you still agree with it? If so, why? If not, why not? Don't forget to include some details in your answer.

The letter

my lord out of the loue i beare ~~you~~ To some of youere freinds i haue a caer of youer preseruacion therfor i would aduyse yowe as yowe Tender youer Lyf To deuys some epscuse To shift of youer aHendance at This parleament for god and man hathe concurred To punishe the wickednes of this Tyme and thinke not slightlye of this aduertisment but reHere youre self into youre contri wheare yowe maye expecT the euent In safti for Thowghe Theare be no apparance of anni stir yet i say they shall receeue a Terrible blowe This parleament and yet they shall not seie who hurts Them This conncel is not To be contemned because it maye do yowe good and can do yowe no harme for The dangere is passed as soonas yowe have burnt the leHer and i hope god wiltgiue yawe The grace To mak good use of it To whose holy proteccion icommend yowe

To the ryght honorable The Lord monteagle

How did the letter arrive?

The official account of what happened was written in the **King's Book**.

'Lord Monteagle was ready to go to supper. At seven of the clock one of his servants was met by a tall man, who delivered a letter. He told him to put it in his master's hands. Lord Monteagle saw the letter was written in an unknown hand, and had no date or signature. He called one of his men to help him to read it.'

👁 ACTIVITIES

1. Find the words in the letter that alarmed James when he read them: 'I say they shall receive a terrible blow this Parliament and yet they shall not see who hurts them.'

2. Work in a group to transcribe the rest of the letter. You may want to give each member of your group different lines to work on.

   (Clue – the letter 's' is usually shown more like an 'f'.)

   Here are some words to help you:
   Line 2 middle – 'preservation'
   Line 3 start – 'advise'
   Line 3 end – 'devise some'
   Line 4 end – 'at this Parliament'
   Line 5 middle – 'concurred'
   Line 8 middle – 'safety'
   Line 9 start – 'appearance of any stir'

What happened next?

Lord Monteagle did not know what to make of the letter. But despite the 'darkness of the night in that season of the year, he went to the palace at Whitehall' and delivered the letter to Robert Cecil. Cecil said, 'that it was likely to be written by a fool or madman.' He decided to wait until the King returned from hunting five days later before doing anything.

James read the letter and decided there was a 'danger by blowing up of powder'. They decided to search Parliament but to wait until the day before it opened.

Unanswered questions...

Monteagle was eating at his house a mile outside London. This was the first time he had eaten there for over a month.

1 How did the tall messenger know he would be at home to read the letter?

2 Edmund Church said that Monteagle already knew there was a letter being sent to him. Edmund Church was a friend of Monteagle's.

3 The government crossed out Monteagle's name if it appeared in the confessions of any of the plotters.

4 Robert Cecil wrote that there were rumours that Monteagle 'was once of this plot of powder, and afterwards betrayed it all to me'.

5 Monteagle made no effort to help his brother-in-law Francis Tresham, who was in prison in the Tower.

6 The servant who helped read the letter was named Thomas Ward. He was related to some of those in the plot and he told them what happened.

7 In a deathbed confession, Tresham denied sending any letter to Monteagle.

Monteagle receiving the letter. A nineteenth-century drawing

ACTIVITIES

Historians have argued over who wrote the letter to Monteagle. But most historians think it was one of these three: Robert Cecil, Francis Tresham or Lord Monteagle himself.

1 Write a few sentences to explain why each of these three might have written the letter.

2 Who you think was most likely to have written the letter? Why do you think this?

Finding out about the plot

1 Using the information from this section about the letter, add more details to the table you began on p65.

2 Which interpretation do you now think is most likely to be true? Do you still agree with the answer and reasons you gave earlier? If you think your answer is still correct, add more evidence to support it. If you have changed your mind, give the theory you now think is true and explain why.

The plot thickens

Other details about the plot

1 The plotters got over 1015 kilograms of gunpowder. At this time you could only make gunpowder with a special licence. The government stored gunpowder in the Tower of London.

2 A war with Spain had just finished and gunpowder was easy to obtain.

3 The plotters were quickly tracked to Holbeach House.

4 The plotters were already being chased because they had tried to steal horses from Warwick Castle.

5 The man who shot Percy and Catesby was given a pension for life.

6 The government gunpowder records for 1604 are missing.

7 Nobody was ever shown the plotters' tunnel.

8 A friend of Robert Cecil's rented the cellar to the plotters.

9 None of the plotters' original confessions were used at the trial. Cecil had copies written to show the court.

10 No witnesses were called at the trial.

11 Confessions were obtained under torture.

Historians have asked many questions about details of the plot. They have also suggested some answers. Sometimes the historians might be right, but not always!

Historian A

'The Catholic plotters were mostly quite young. They were desperate. They thought they had nothing to lose by trying to kill the king. Many of them had been in the Earl of Essex's rebellion against Elizabeth I in 1607. If they were prepared to revolt then, why not during James's reign as well?'

Historian C

'Cecil probably heard about the plot from one of his spies. He just kept an eye on it but did not act. Cecil was not involved in the plot. But he knew that it would be more dramatic if he pretended to uncover it at the last moment.'

Historian B

'Robert Cecil was the king's spymaster. He wanted to give James an excuse to persecute the Catholics. He was behind the plot from the start. He made sure they could get gunpowder. He made sure they had somewhere under Parliament to put it.'

Historian D

Somebody in the plot betrayed it. We will never know for sure who or why. This meant that the government was lucky not to be blown up. The plot might not have succeeded completely. But Fawkes and the others may have managed to kill the king.'

What were the consequences of the plot?

Most English Catholics were horrified when they heard about the plot. They did not like paying fines but they believed they should still be loyal to the king. This did not stop the government passing new laws. Catholics were no longer allowed to become officers in the army or navy. They could not become lawyers. They were not allowed to vote in elections (this lasted until 1829). From 1606 on, Catholics were treated with increased suspicion. They were blamed for starting the Great Fire of London. Other supposed Catholic plots were uncovered over the next century.

Stretching a Catholic prisoner on the rack

Finding out about the plot

So, who really was to blame for the Gunpowder Plot? It is now time to decide whether you think the Gunpowder Plot was:

a) a Catholic conspiracy, or

b) a Cecil set-up

1 Work in pairs. One of you must argue that the plot was a Catholic conspiracy. The other person must argue that it was a Cecil set-up. Use the evidence that you have collected in your table and your answers to the activities in the unit to help you. Remember, your arguments should be detailed and based on the evidence!

2 Present your arguments to each other. Which do you find most convincing? Why? Do you want to revise your ideas?

3 Now write your story of the Gunpowder Plot. The story should give your interpretation of who was really to blame for the plot. Here are some tips to help you:

- Decide what your theory of the plot is.

- How will you persuade your reader that your theory is the right one?

   – What evidence can you use to back up your arguments?

   – What words or phrases can you use to persuade your reader? E.g.
     The evidence shows that...
     The only possible explanation is...
     It must be true that...

- How will you persuade your reader that the other theories are wrong?

   – How will you deal with the evidence that *doesn't* support your argument? Will you leave it out of your story altogether? Or will you try and give possible explanations for it?

   – What words or phrases can you use in your argument?
     On the other hand...
     Then again...

- Remember to think about the structure of your story:

   – Does it have an introduction? You might want to give some background to the plot.

   – How are you going to organise your paragraphs? What information will you include in each one?

   – Does it have a conclusion? You should use this section to sum up your argument.

   – Try to make sure that your story reads chronologically (i.e. that all the events are in the right order!)

| 1603 | 1610 | 1620 | 1630 | 1640 | 1642 |

1603	1608	1611	1614	1621	1625	1629
James I becomes King of England	Parliament stops James from increasing customs duties	James dismisses Parliament	Parliament refuses to grant James any new taxes	James and Parliament quarrel over who Charles should marry	Charles I becomes king and marries a Catholic princess	Charles dismisses Parliament and rules alone for 11 years

For King or for Parliament?

The final challenge

On 3 January 1642, Charles I gave orders for the arrest of five **Members of Parliament**. The **House of Commons** refused to surrender them. On the advice of his Queen, Charles decided to use force to capture them. 'Go and pull those rogues out by the ears, or never see my face again' she is supposed to have ordered him.

Charles I entering Parliament to arrest the five MPs. Painted in the eighteenth century

1633	1634	1637	1640	1641	Jan 1642	Aug 1642
William Laud becomes Archbishop of Canterbury	Ship Money is extended to the whole country	Charles tries to force Scotland to use the English Prayer Book	Charles recalls Parliament to raise money to fight the Scots	The Grand Remonstrance	Charles fails to arrest five Members of Parliament	Charles raises his standard in Nottingham

At about 3 o'clock the following afternoon a messenger arrived at Westminster to speak to John Pym, who was the leader of the five members in the Commons. The messenger told Pym that the King, accompanied by a party of soldiers, would be arriving shortly to arrest the five members. Pym immediately informed the Commons, and asked the **Speaker** to allow him and the four others to leave. But, to make sure that the King did break into the Commons chamber, they stayed until the last possible moment.

Leaving his soldiers at the door, the King entered the Commons, taking off his hat as a mark of respect as he did so. The members stood up and removed their hats too. Charles then asked for each of the five members by name. He was answered with silence. Even the Speaker refused to say whether they were present. Borrowing the Speaker's chair for a moment, he looked around, noting significant empty spaces. 'I see all my birds have flown,' he remarked, and left. Pym and the other four members were by now on a barge escaping down the River Thames into the City of London.

That night barricades were set up across London, cannon were dragged into firing positions and water was boiled for throwing on the heads of royal soldiers. When the King ventured out in his coach, he was surrounded by an angry mob. They were shouting 'Privilege! Privilege!' They meant the privileges and liberties of Parliament.

Six days later, the King, his family and his court left London and headed north. It had become too dangerous for them to stay. Charles tried to rally armed support for his cause. Finally, on 22 August 1642, he raised his standard in a field near Nottingham. The Civil War had begun...

ACTIVITIES

1. Why do you think Pym wanted the King to break into the House of Commons?

2. What does the story tell you about the King's view of the House of Commons?

3. What does it tell you about the House of Commons' view of the King?

But why had relations between the King and Parliament become so bad? How did it all start? Why did Civil War break out in England in 1642?

NEW WORDS

House of Commons
the place where the elected representatives of the people meet

Members of Parliament (MPs)
People elected or chosen to sit in the House of Commons

Speaker
the person in charge in the Commons

The **background**

Kings had always called for advice from a council of important and trusted men. During the Middle Ages they sometimes also called a Parliament.

Monarch

Parliament

Lords. *Important landowners and churchmen*

Commons. *Elected from local areas. Two knights were elected from each shire by wealthy landowners. Two burgesses were chosen from each town*

How Parliament worked at the end of the sixteenth century

The origins of Parliament

The name comes from the French word *parler* meaning 'to talk' or 'to discuss'. At first a Parliament could be held anywhere the king chose. Lords and important churchmen were called. There were also representatives from the localities (in French *communes*), who were known as the Commons. They were knights elected by richer farmers and **burgesses** chosen by wealthy merchants and tradesmen in the towns. By the late fourteenth century, being a Member of Parliament (MP) was considered an honour. MPs had extra privileges, such as freedom from arrest while on parliamentary business.

By the Tudor period Parliament always met at Westminster. But this was only when the monarch called them, and then often only for a few weeks. Now the Lords met separately from the Commons and new laws and taxes had to be agreed by both groups. The king or queen could demand taxes only if Parliament agreed.

The importance of Parliament gradually increased, particularly after Henry VIII used Parliament to help make himself head of the Church. During the reign of Elizabeth the Commons sometimes tried to make use of this new influence. But as Elizabeth's final speech to Parliament shows, she knew how to handle them.

> **'Though God hath raised me high yet this I count the glory of my crown, that I have reigned with your loves.'**

Look back

Do you remember how King John tried to sort out his differences with his Barons by signing Magna Carta in 1215? See *History First 1066–1500*, pages 62–63 for details.

NEW WORDS

- **Burgesses**
  representatives of a town or borough

EXTENSION ACTIVITY

Make a diagram or chart showing the differences between Parliament in 1603 and Parliament today. You may need to do some extra research.

SOURCE B

Elizabeth meeting Parliament

SOURCE C

Monarch	Number of Parliaments	Total sessions	Reign
Henry VII	7	7	1485 – 1509
Henry VIII	9	28	1509 – 1547
Edward VI	3	6	1547 – 1553
Mary I	4	5	1553 – 1558
Elizabeth I	12	17	1558 – 1603

ACTIVITIES

1. How did Parliament change between the Middle Ages and 1603?

2. Use Source C to try and work out which monarch made the most use of Parliament. Remember to look at the number of years they reigned before you explain how you reached your answer.

Why couldn't the king and Parliament agree?

Parliament had usually allowed Henry VIII and Elizabeth to do what they wanted. When Elizabeth died in 1603, she was succeeded by James I and VI of Scotland, the son of Mary, Queen of Scots. He was determined to make sure that it did not argue with him. But Parliament did not like all his ideas...

Quarrels with James I

James believed that he had been chosen by God to be king. He even told Parliament that God himself called kings 'gods'! This idea was known as the 'Divine Right of Kings'. It meant that no one could argue with a king because that would be the same as arguing with God!

But the members of the House of Commons disagreed. They were not about to hand over all their power to him. They had one weapon they could use against James – and they did. They kept him short of money.

James needed more money than Elizabeth to run the country. Prices were rising and large debts remained from the old Queen's wars. One of James's incomes was from **customs duties** on goods coming into the country. When he tried to raise these in 1606, he was told he could not collect this money unless Parliament agreed. James was furious. In 1611 he told the Members of Parliament to go home!

In 1614 James called Parliament again as he needed money. It met for eight weeks, but the Commons refused to grant James any new taxes. Since then this has been known as the Addled Parliament as it was so ineffective.

During the 22 years of James's reign, Parliament was called 4 times and met for just 9 sessions.

James I

The King preferred to use his friends to help him run the country, but some of these made him even more unpopular with Parliament. He also found other ways of raising money, such as selling people titles and more monopolies.

In 1621, James called Parliament for the last time. But immediately there were arguments. James wanted his son to marry a Spanish princess who was Catholic. If a Catholic married the future king of England, their children might be brought up as Catholics. Then England might have a Catholic monarch again. This was the last thing that the House of Commons, which was strongly Puritan, wanted.

ACTIVITIES

1. The table below shows the main reasons for the quarrels between King James and Parliament. Fill in the remaining two columns using the information above.

Cause of argument	King James's view	Parliament's view
Divine Right of Kings		
Money		
Religion		

2. Which argument do you think was the most serious from the King's point of view? Why?

3. Which do you think was the most serious from Parliament's point of view? Why?

4. Could a compromise be reached? How?

Quarrels with Charles I

Charles I

Charles became king on the death of his father, James I, in 1625. The marriage to the Spanish princess never happened. Instead, in the same year, he married the 15 year-old daughter of Henry IV of France, Henrietta Maria. She, too, was Catholic. Parliament was angry. It was a bad start to his reign. And things did not improve...

NEW WORDS

Customs duties
taxes on goods brought into the country

Why was England at war in 1642?

I suppose a lot of it goes back to the arguments the King had with Parliament over money. Charles needed money when he became king in 1625. Only Parliament can give permission for a king to collect new taxes. But some MPs began to make demands on the King before they would agree to help him.

In the end Charles got fed up and decided to rule England without Parliament. He thought that kings should be able to rule as they wanted. Not surprisingly, Parliament disagreed!

King Charles ruled for 11 years without calling Parliament. He had just enough money to get by because we were at peace then. But he upset a lot of people by trying to raise money without Parliament's consent. **Ship Money** was the biggest cause of trouble.

His Majesty also upset some people over the religious changes he made. As you know, our king had married a French Catholic princess back in 1625, and many of us thought he really wanted to make England a Catholic country again.

He also made William Laud Archbishop of Canterbury. Laud wanted to make sure that everyone worshipped in the same way. He made changes to the churches, so they looked more like Catholic ones. They were much fancier inside. This infuriated many people, especially the Puritans. They thought the church was not Protestant enough and needed more reform. Many MPs were **Puritans**. Charles hated Puritans!

Things really went downhill in 1637 when King Charles tried to get the Scots to use the English Prayer Book. The Scottish people had their own church, and decided to fight to keep their religion the way it was. They rioted wherever the Prayer Book was used. Charles couldn't afford to raise an army to fight back so he was forced to call Parliament again in 1640.

It was the moment MPs had been waiting for. They disagreed with the way Charles was ruling and were determined to limit his power. They made a lot of demands on Charles. He did give in to most of them. Archbishop Laud was even put in prison.

It still did not look to me like there would be a war then. But some MPs wanted Parliament to have even more power. I read the **Grand Remonstrance** they published. They demanded that the church be reformed, and that Parliament control the army and appointment of royal ministers. No one had ever dared to attack the king's powers like this before! Some MPs thought they had gone too far and the King began to get more support.

I believe that the final straw was when Charles went to Parliament with soldiers to arrest five of the MPs who were giving him the most trouble. They escaped and were made heroes in London. Charles had to leave the city. Attempts to solve the quarrel failed. Within a few months we knew there would be a **civil war**.

ACTIVITIES

1. Why do you think Charles quarrelled with parliament? Make a list of all the reasons you can find.

2. How similar were Charles's problems with Parliament to those his father faced?

3. Make a list of any of Charles's actions that made the situation worse.

4. Make a list of the causes of the war. For each one, decide whether it was a long term or short term cause.

5. Which of the causes do you think were the most important?

NEW WORDS

Civil war
a war between people within the same country

Grand Remonstrance
a long document drawn up by Parliament condemning Charles's government

Puritans
extreme Protestants who formed a powerful political party in Parliament

Ship Money
a special tax to help pay for the navy. Previously it had been paid only by ports, who needed the protection of the navy. Charles tried to extend it to the whole country

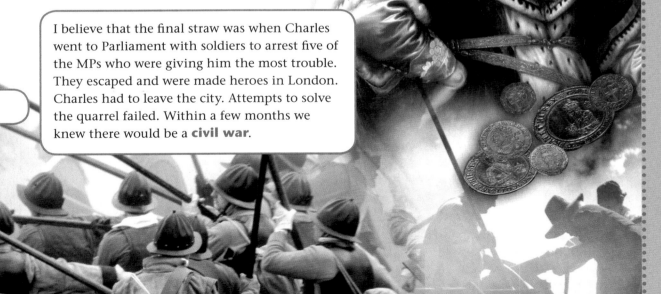

1642   1648

22 Aug 1642	23 Oct 1642	2 Jul 1644	Feb 1645	14 Jun 1645	1645
King Charles I raises his standard at Nottingham	The Battle of Edgehill; start of the First Civil War	The Battle of Marston Moor; a Parlimentary victory	Parliament forms the New Model Army	The Battle of Naseby; a Parliamentary victory	The Leveller movement emerges

How did the Civil War affect ordinary people?

One wound a day and two on Sundays

The gunshot that you meet as you charge the enemy is aimed low. The musket ball striking your leg feels like a sledgehammer. Lying on the grass you await your fate at the hands of the surgeon.

Not being an officer you do not qualify for a place in a church or a tavern. As a common soldier you rate a sheep fold. Operating tables are not used. You sit in a chair under which is shovelled ash to soak up the blood. The fold reeks of blood, urine, vomit and other nasty smells.

You consider your wounds. It's common knowledge that shot wounds develop **bad humours**. Any real chance of your survival will depend on the training of the surgeon. For a wound to your leg, what will the surgeon do? All surgeons agree. The only treatment for a gunshot wound that breaks the leg bone is **amputation** within 48 hours. This will be your only chance of survival. Two surgeon's mates secure you in the chair and pass tools to the surgeon. If you are lucky the surgeon may have studied the work of Pare, a famous French surgeon. He might wash his hands. To reduce or prevent infection the leg will be cut through healthy **tissue**, mid thigh. The larger of the mates pins you by the shoulders. The second assistant applies a pillow to suffocate you. Pare was a firm believer in relieving pain.

Suffocation would leave you half dead and unconscious. Whilst you were unaware, the surgeon would swiftly cut off the injured leg. The wound may be painted in a soothing mixture of egg white, rose oil and turpentine to reduce infection. Time of operation, 10 minutes. Chance of survival, 25%.

This is what might have happened to
anyone unlucky enough to be wounded
during battle. But the English Civil War
affected many more than those injured
or killed. In this unit, you will try to
decide how much the lives of ordinary
people were changed by war.

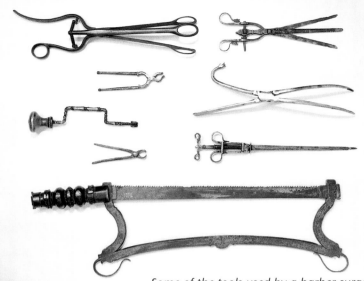

Some of the tools used by a barber surgeon

ACTIVITIES

1. Write down five adjectives that give your reaction to the story.

2. How would you expect a leg wound to be treated today? Are there any similarities?

3. The story opposite is a fictional account. Try to list at least three types of sources the writer might have used to get his evidence.

4. How would you go about checking if the story is historically accurate?

NEW WORDS

Amputation
 cut off a part of the body
Bad humours
 became septic
Tissue
 flesh

Diaries and history

By 1642, when the Civil War started, about one in four people could read and write. We have quite a lot of evidence about what was going on from letters written at the time. Printing presses were quite common, and the pamphlets, cartoons and official documents they produced give us clues about what people were thinking. This was a time when more broadsheets (early newspapers) were beginning to appear.

We also have diaries. For a long time some people had kept journals, recording the work of their businesses. But during the seventeenth century personal diary writing became popular. Most of those who kept these diaries did not intend them to be read by other people. This means they provide a unique type of evidence about the period. They describe everyday details and give an idea of what people were thinking and feeling at the time. You will look at one diary like this in the next unit.

Diaries give us a lot of detailed evidence about the past

Finding out about the Civil War

The final task for this unit is to write a short guide for people who want to become Civil War re-enactors. They are people who gather together to re-enact the events in the Civil War. You will need to make sure your guide includes enough information so that the re-enactors can look and behave as authentically as possible!

To help you, you will be keeping a diary as you work through the unit. Diaries from the period are an important source of information for re-enactors. They often provide lots of detail about the period. This helps re-enactors to make their costumes, weapons and battles as authentic as possible.

In your diary, you will gather evidence about what life was like for ordinary people during the Civil War. You will need to use your diary to write your re-enactment guide.

When you are writing the diary, you will need to make sure that you write it from the point of view of someone living at the time. Try to think about how people at the time might have seen and understood things.

Use this list as a 'toolkit' for writing your diary:

- You must do careful research to get your facts right.
- You must think about how people at the time would have felt as events occurred.
- You must use the past tense to describe what has just happened.
- You must use the present tense to describe what you are doing and feeling.
- You must use the future tense to describe your hopes and plans for the future.

You are going to write your diary as if you are an ordinary soldier. To be able to write you are probably not a farm labourer. More likely you are from a craftsman's family such as a tailor, carpenter or stonemason. Most likely you are a man, but some women did pretend to be men and join the army.

Choose a name and occupation for yourself and write your first entry, explaining who you are and giving information about your family, job, home, etc. You might find some of the information on the next page helpful.

Diary help

You will also need some extra information to help you make your diary more authentic to the time.

Common words

You might want to include some of the words that people would have used at the time. Here are some examples:

divers – many
poke – pocket or large bag
tarry – wait
peck – food
master/mistress – Mr/Mrs

physic – medicine
prithee – I pray you
jakes – privy (toilet)
good morrow – hello

If you need to use some 'bad language' try:

rip me   burn my vitals   zooks

Good morrow mistress Smith, whither away?

Good day 'ee master Fielding. I go to the village.

Fare you well, mistress.

Food

The daily ration for a soldier was supposed to be 2 pounds of bread, 1 pound of cheese or meat (usually beef), a bottle of wine or two bottles of beer.

Common names in 1642

John	Thomas
Walter	Hugh
Anne	Susanna
Joyce	Abigail
Samuel	Nathaniel
Simon	Jonas
Grace	Martha
Temperance	Charity

Money, wages and prices

Pounds (£), shillings (s) and pence (d) were the main types of money in use.
There were 12 pennies in a shilling and 20 shillings in a pound.
The smallest coin was a 'farthing', a quarter of a penny.
£1 in 1642 could buy about the same as £75 today.
A labourer earned up to 1s a day.
A foot soldier earned about 4s a week.
1d could buy two pints of ale or three loaves of bread.
6d could buy two lean chickens or some wine.
1s could buy a lean pig or a fat goose.
3s could buy a hat.
9s could buy a pair of boots.

Choosing sides

King Charles raised his standard at Nottingham in August 1642. He was calling for everyone to support him against Parliament. All over the country people had to decide if they would get involved, or which side to join.

Which side a person supported depended on a number of things. At the start of the war the King could rely on the support of the West, Midlands and North. Most of Cornwall and Wales stayed loyal to the King throughout the war. They provided many of the best soldiers in his infantry. Parliament had more supporters in the South and East, and, crucially, in London. Of course, in many areas, there was not such a neat division of support. The war split the loyalties of localities, towns and even families.

Raising an army

Able-bodied men between 15 and 60 could be called upon to fight. Some already belonged to trained bands. These were ordinary people who spent some time training with weapons.

Some men had no choice about what side to support. In Lancashire, the Royalists forced local men to attack Parliament's garrison at Bolton.

SOURCE A

The drums beat up to call together the band. The captain demanded of their willingness to serve the king. Then they all threw up their hats and cried 'God save the king' and many of them again 'For the king, For the king'.

A letter from Herefordshire, 14 July 1642

SOURCE B

The rear was brought up with soldiers that were ordered to shoot those as lagged behind. So the poor countrymen were in a dilemma of death. Either by the troopers if they went not on, or by the shot of the town if they did.

A modern historian

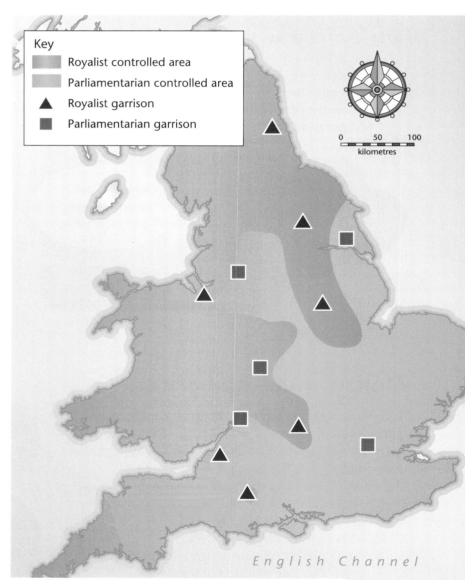

Map of England and Wales, showing the areas under Royalist and Parliamentarian control in 1643

SOURCE C

A cartoon of the time

Here is an extract from a diary by Lucy Hutchison.
It describes how at the start of the war in 1642 different
counties decided which side to support.

SOURCE D

**In many places, there were fierce disputes, almost to
blood. For every county had the civil war, more or less,
within itself. Some counties were in the beginning
wholly for the parliament some wholly for the king.**

Lucy Hutchinson, Memoirs of Colonel Hutchinson

In fact Lucy wrote this soon after her husband died in
1664. He had fought on Parliament's side during the war.
She wrote as if it were her husband's own words, but it is
thought she used her own diary to remember the details.

ACTIVITIES

1 From sources A to D pick the one that **best**
   matches each of these statements:

   • Some people did not want to be involved
   • Different areas supported different sides
   • Some people were keen to fight
   • Both sides had equal support

2 Pick the source that gives the best clue about
   how people chose sides. Give at least one
   reason for your choice.

3 Copy and complete one of these sentences:

   – Some types of sources are more useful than
     others because…
   – All types of sources can be useful because…

Finding out about the Civil War

1 Make a draft of a diary entry for 25 August 1642
   where you decide if you are going to support king or
   Parliament. Include some of the details above in your
   writing and try to show that it is a difficult decision. You
   can improve your work after you have looked at the next
   section. You could start with: 'I have decided to join the
   army. I want to support my king because …'

2 Write a diary entry about leaving home to join the army.
   Use the future tense for some of your writing to talk
   about your hopes and worries. Include some dialogue
   with your family or friends about why you have chosen
   to go. You could write about buying some things to take
   with you.

Oh to be a **soldier!**

Civil War armies had cavalry (soldiers on horseback), infantry (foot soldiers) and artillery (cannons).

You are going to be an infantryman. That means you will become one of these two types of soldier: a pikeman or a musketeer.

The main job of the pikemen was to protect the musketeers from enemy cavalry. There were usually two musketeers to every pikeman. Soldiers had to be well trained to work together. Handling the five metre long pikes was difficult and the pikemen had to respond quickly to orders.

A pikeman

- Pot helmet
- Five metre ash pike
- Iron corselet
- Leather **snapsack** containing food and spare clothes
- Short sword
- **Tassets**
- Woollen **breeches**
- Wool stockings

A musketeer

- Knitted woollen cap
- Matchlock musket
- Wooden tubes of gunpowder
- Powder horn
- Leather shoes

Look back

Look back to *History First 1066–1500*, pages 109–11.

1. Compare the armour and weapons shown here with those used in the Wars of the Roses. Make two lists: one of similarities, the other of differences.

2. Do you think warfare had advanced between 1485 and 1642? You will need to give some reasons for your answer.

Finding out about the Civil War

1. Decide if you want to be a pikeman or a musketeer.

2. Add an entry to your diary about your weapons and your training.

Life on the move

Being in the army meant accepting a life on the move. Many soldiers were away from home for the first time. They either slept in camps or were **billeted** with local families wherever they were. Most ordinary soldiers had to march everywhere on foot. Progress was often painfully slow, particularly as the larger weapons and equipment frequently got stuck in the country lanes.

Mark Turnbull is an English Civil War re-enactor. In this piece of fiction he gives lots of details about life in the army.

'I march now for Edgehill, angry and worried. Never have I left my village for more than a few miles, and now I find myself so far away from my family and livelihood.

In the scorching heat, I am dressed in a plain white shirt, covered by a thick coat. I wear breeches to my knees, with wool stockings below that, to my shoes. I have no sword, I had no money to buy one and I was not given the full quota of armour. I only have a battered back and breast plate, 30 years old, and a helmet. If this isn't enough, I carry a 16-foot ash wood pole in my gloved hands, with an iron spike on the top. This clumsy weapon, a pike, knocks me off balance when I march, as though I am drunk.

That reminds me of food, my rations are bad. I have not eaten since yesterday dinner, when we lost a skirmish. Now we are organised again, I expect my daily rations of 2 pounds of bread, one pound of meat and 2 bottles of beer. I had the choice between meat and cheese, but meat is more filling.'

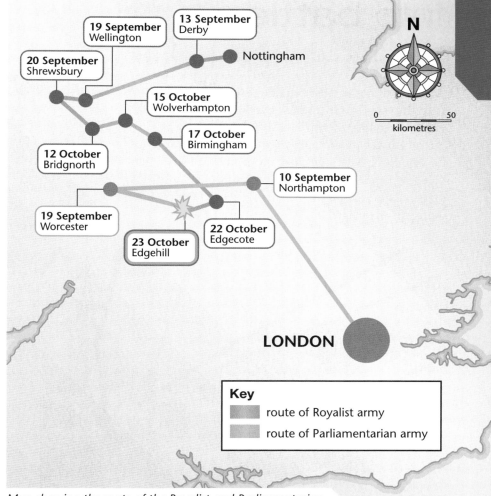

Map showing the route of the Royalist and Parliamentarian armies on their way to the Battle of Edgehill

ACTIVITIES

1. List anything in the passage that suggests the soldier was not properly prepared for war.

2. Is there anything in the passage that could not easily have been learned from contemporary sources?

NEW WORDS

- **Billeted**
  lodged with
- **Breeches**
  trousers
- **Snapsack**
  bag
- **Tassets**
  armour protecting the area below the waist

Finding out about the Civil War

Use the information in this section to write a diary entry about army life. Make sure you include details about places soldiers were billeted on the march. What sort of things do you and the other soldiers talk about? Are their concerns the same as yours?

Into battle
The Battle of Edgehill

The first major battle of the English Civil War was also the biggest. On 23 October 1642 the two armies met at Edgehill, in Warwickshire. The King was marching towards London and Parliament wanted to stop him. Both sides had about 14,000 men. The fighting began in the afternoon and went on until dark. Historians give differing figures for the numbers killed in the battle, but it was at least 1,500.

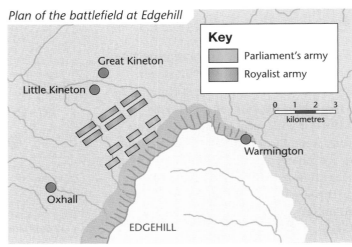

Plan of the battlefield at Edgehill

Key
- Parliament's army
- Royalist army

Great Kineton
Little Kineton
Warmington
Oxhall
EDGEHILL

Pikemen

Evidence about the battle

SOURCE A

We charged them with some loss from their pikes though very little from their muskets; but not being able to break them. We had retreated to our former station when a body of horse appeared advancing towards us. We fired at them only wounding one man through the hand, which fell out very happily, they being of our own army.

An account by Edmund Ludlow, who fought in Parliament's army

SOURCE B

We gave fire with our cannon and then charged them with both wings of our horse. Upon our approach they gave fire with their cannon but finding that did not frighten the King's horse, they all began to run away and we followed them for 4 miles [6.5 kilometres] together. The left wing did the same. A great many of them saved their lives by calling out For God and King Charles.

A Royalist account of the battle

The enemy foot came up to the King's men, and by their courage reached the King's standard, the bearer was killed and it was taken. Night made them sound the retreat. The king was master of the field.

A Royalist newsletter account of the battle

SOURCE C

This only will we say, some of both sides did extremely well, and others did as ill, and deserve to be hanged. But God alone is to be praised, who fought with us, and for us, and gave the Victory unto his Servants. The King's Foot are either slain, or most of them run away.

Part of Parliament's official account of the battle

Cavalry and foot soldiers

ACTIVITIES

1 Here are some statements made by historians about the battle. Pick out the ones you think are supported by the sources.

- It took the Royalists over six hours to draw up their army in battle formation.
- The battle began with an artillery duel.
- The Royalist cavalry on the right wing charged. Parliament's cavalry lost their nerve and fled.
- A bitter struggle raged as the two armies came to **push of pike**.
- On the left wing Parliament's horse were scattered.
- Some of Parliament's horse fell back only to be fired on by their own men who mistook them for Royalists.
- At the end of the battle the two sides had fought to a standstill.

2 All these statements are true. Why are some not supported by the sources?

3 So which side won the battle? You have three choices:
a) I think the King won because...
b) I think Parliament won because...
c) I think the battle was a draw because...

Pick the answer that you think is correct. Complete your answer, including at least three details from the sources.

NEW WORDS

Push of pike
hand to hand fighting

Finding out about the Civil War

1 You were there – add an entry about the battle to your diary. This should be a detailed piece of writing. Here is a small 'toolkit' of things to include or think about:
- Lining up for the battle
- Flags and drums
- Gunpowder smoke
- Use the five senses
- Use strong adjectives

2 Now look back at the story that started this unit. Use this to help you write a diary entry for the day after the Battle of Edgehill when you are helping a surgeon tend the wounded.

89

The war and **civilians**

The English Civil War that began in 1642 was, in fact, three separate civil wars. But the first war, which lasted until 1646, was the longest and most important. It included 20 major battles, many **skirmishes** and over 30 sieges. There was also fighting in Ireland, Wales and Scotland.

It was not just soldiers who were affected by the war. **Civilians** were also involved. Of course, not everybody was affected by the war in the same way.

A lot of people's experience of the war depended on where they lived. Troops often went unpaid and had to take 'free quarter' in local towns and villages. Not surprisingly many people who lived in areas where armies were moving through resented the way soldiers **plundered** their possessions and were billeted on them. In some areas groups of people banded together and were prepared to fight against both sides to keep the troops out. These groups were known as Clubmen. One estimate is that 600 Clubmen were killed during the war.

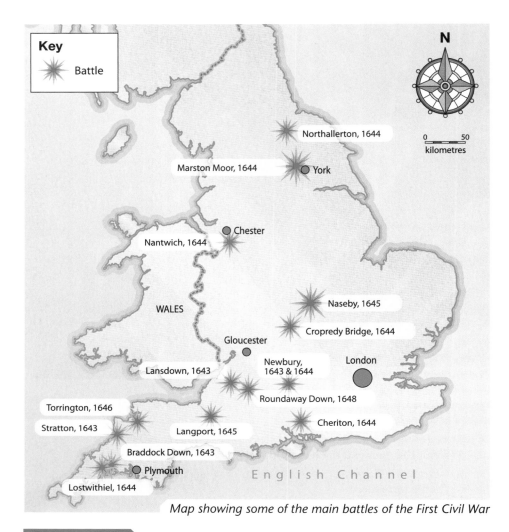

Map showing some of the main battles of the First Civil War

SOURCE A

Many civilians were at one time or another plundered of their possessions. The English language reflected this important change. Although the word 'plunder' was first used in 1632 it became commonplace a decade later. A pamphlet in 1642 described how after the king's army captured Brentford 'they plundered it without any respect of persons'.

In The Civil Wars, John Kenyon and Jane Ohlmeyer (editors) (1998)

ACTIVITIES

1. What does the map tell you about the extent of the fighting?

2. Are there any parts of the country that appear free from fighting?

NEW WORDS

Civilians
people who are not soldiers
Plundered
robbed
Skirmishes
small localised battles

Finding out about the Civil War

Add a short diary entry that shows how local people react to you being billeted on them.

The **weaker vessel?**

'The weaker vessel' was an expression sometimes used about women in the seventeenth century. This was a time when women were supposed to obey their husbands, only widows could control their own property and no women could vote. However, this did not mean they were not affected by the war. Women played a vital role, and not just as civilians. They also supported the military effort.

Life with the army

A few women dressed as men and fought in the army. Below is part of a letter reporting one such woman.

SOURCE A

A young person is discovered to be a woman; her name she saith is Ann Dimack of Lincolnshire. She saith she fell in love with one John Evison. She put herself into a man's **habit**, and they went as two brothers. John died and she listed herself for a soldier in his name.

Most often these women seem to have joined the army to be with their husbands. One such woman known as 'Mr Clarke' had a song written about her.

SOURCE B

Her husband was a soldier, and to the wars did go
And she would be his comrade, the truth of all is so,
She put on man's **apparel** and bore him company
As many in the army for truth can testify

'Mr Clarke' was discovered only when she gave birth. While pregnant she had put her size down to 'strong beer and tobacco'.

Other songs of the time record that women in the army took part in the fighting.

SOURCE C

With musket on her shoulder, her part she acted then,
And everyone supposed that she had been a man;
Her **bandoliers** about her neck and sword hanged by her side
In many brave adventures her **valour** has been tried

Many other women followed their husbands to war as 'camp followers'. Armies did not have professional support and it was women who cooked, sewed, washed clothes and cared for the wounded.

A woman soldier

NEW WORDS

Apparel
   clothes
Bandoliers
   shoulder belt for gun cartridges
Habit
   dress
Valour
   courage

ACTIVITIES

1. Suggest some reasons why women might try to join the army.

2. What do the songs suggest about attitudes to women in the army?

3. How important do you think women camp followers were to the armies? Explain your answer.

Life in camp

Life under siege

Women didn't have to be in the army to experience the war at first hand. There were more sieges than battles during the war, and as civilians, many women helped to defend towns against attack.

Thousands of women helped build an earth wall 5.5 metres high and 18 kilometres long to protect London from attack by the Royalists. This poem was written about them:

SOURCE A

From ladies down to Oyster wenches
Laboured the pioneers in the trenches
Fallen to pickaxes and tools
And helped the men dig like moles.

At the siege of Basing House, women threw stones down at the attacking Parliamentarian soldiers. At Lyme Regis women put out fires, stood guard at night and reloaded soldiers' muskets. They are also recorded as firing on the enemy. A serving girl shot and killed a Parliamentary captain at the siege of Withenshaw House. At the siege of Worcester, several women lost their lives acting as snipers while the men got some rest.

This piece of fiction writing describes a famous event during the siege of Gloucester, when a 27 kilogram shell fell into the street:

SOURCE B

The women scattered like a flock of hens, throwing themselves down behind walls and under carts. There was a piercing whistle and a gust of hot air as the enormous iron ball hurtled down and buried itself up to its hissing neck in a heap of clay.

Ella peered through her fingers as the dust settled. The great ball had stuck fast in the heavy soil, the sparking fuse cut far too long. It hissed and popped, giving off a cloud of angry sparks and smoke. Ella rolled over and leaped to her feet, snatched up the nearest pail and threw the water over the hellish bomb. The fuse was extinguished in an instant. It was no more than a useless lump of iron.

From King's Crow Men, Nicholas Carter (1997)

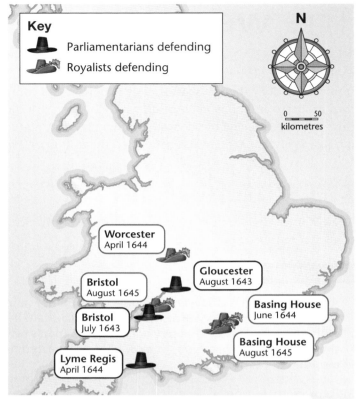

Key
Parliamentarians defending
Royalists defending

N

0   50
kilometres

Worcester
April 1644

Gloucester
August 1643

Bristol
August 1645

Basing House
June 1644

Bristol
July 1643

Basing House
August 1645

Lyme Regis
April 1644

Map of England and Wales, showing some of the major sieges of the war

ACTIVITIES

1. Make a list of the ways in which women helped to defend towns against attack.

2. Why were women so involved in defending towns from sieges?

Charlotte Tremouille tearing up the summons to surrender Latham House

Life at home

For other women, the war may have been less dramatic, but it was no less traumatic. Most women stayed at home, trying to support their families, waiting for their husbands to return. With men away fighting, there were fewer people to farm the land, and there were several harvest failures during the war. Many families faced severe hardships, even if they were nowhere near the fighting. Many women never discovered what happened to their husbands who went away to war. In some cases, they were left penniless.

SOURCE A

Most dear and loving husband,

I remember unto you, hoping that you are in good health. I pray you to come home if you can come safely. I do marvel that I cannot hear from you as well other neighbours do. I do desire to hear from you as soon as you can. I am a lone woman; I thought you would never have leave me thus long.

Your loving wife, Susan Rodway.

Ever praying for you till death I depart.

A letter from a soldier's wife

This poem, written in 1646, gives one view of women's contribution during the Civil War:

SOURCE B

Women they say the Weaker Vessel are,
If so, it is a paradox to men
That those who never trained up in war
So often should obtain victory.

Royalist propaganda showing soldiers attacking 'Popish' images in a church

ACTIVITIES

1. Make a list of all the different activities carried out by women during the Civil War.

2. Do you think women played an important part in the war?

Parliamentary propaganda about the cruelty of the Royalists

Finding out about the Civil War

Add at least two entries to your diary about a siege. Make sure it includes something about the role of women in the action.

Add an entry about the family you have left behind. How are they surviving without you?

People, politics and the war

Living in the upheaval of civil war led many people to think more about their lives. Some began to wonder about their rights. Parliament was prepared to fight the king to limit his power and to defend its rights. If Parliament could ask ordinary people to fight and risk their lives for Parliament's rights, then perhaps that meant it was time for wider changes?

The Levellers

One of the groups demanding change was known as the Levellers. The Levellers wanted peaceful change. They also believed people should be free to worship God how they wished. The Levellers campaigned by producing pamphlets for ordinary people to read. They started their own newspaper, called *The Moderate*. They used petitions to try to persuade the country's leaders that their ideas were just.

One famous Leveller pamphlet was written by John Lilbourne. It was called *An Agreement of the People*.

'The World turn'd upside down' from a pamphlet published in 1647

AN
AGREEMENT
OF THE
PEOPLE
FOR
A firme and prefent Peace , upon grounds of common-right and free—dome;

As it was propofed by the Agents of the five Regiments of Horfe; and fince by the generall approbation of the Army, offered to the joynt concurrence of all the free COMMONS of ENGLAND.

The Names of the Regiments which have already appeared for the Cafe, of *The Cafe of the Army truly ftated*, and for this prefent Agreement, VIZ.

1. Gen. Regiment.
2. Life-Guard.
3. Lieut.Gen.Regiment.
4. Com.Gen.Regiment.
5. Col. Whaleyes Reg.
6. Col. Rickes Reg.
7. Col. Fleetwoods Reg.
8. Col. Harrifons Reg.
9. Col. Twiftdens Reg.

Of Horfe

1. Gen. Regiment.
2. Col.Sir Hardreffe Wallers Reg.
3. Col. Lamberts Reg.
4. Col. Rainsboroughs Regiment.
5. Col. Overtons Reg.
6. Col. Lilburns Reg.
7. Col. Backflers Reg.

Of Foot

Printed Anno Dom. 1647.

Here are some of the ideas contained in *An Agreement of the People*:

- Elections to Parliament every two years
- Parliament has ultimate authority in the country
- Religious toleration
- No conscription into the army
- No one should be above the law
- The law should be applied equally.

The Levellers also wanted 'universal manhood suffrage'. They thought every man should be able to vote. But this did not include servants, or those living on charity. They made no mention of women's voting rights. This did not stop some women supporting the Levellers.

Levellers wore sea-green ribbons to show their sympathies. They had a lot of popular support, particularly from ordinary men in the army who had been fighting for Parliament. But soldiers were not allowed to vote for it. Leading Levellers were often threatened or imprisoned. After Lilbourne and three other Levellers were arrested in March 1649, part of the army **mutinied**, demanding their release. In May many of the mutineers were captured and condemned to death. They drew lots to see who would die. Three of them were shot in Burford churchyard.

ACTIVITIES

1. Pick out and write down the Leveller ideas in this list:
   - Violent revolution
   - Votes for women
   - Abolition of the monarchy
   - Trial by jury
   - Religious freedom
   - Forcing men to join the army
   - Elections every five years.

2. Why might the Levellers not demand the vote for servants and women?

3. How many of the Levellers' ideas are in place today?

NEW WORDS

Mutinied
   rebelled against

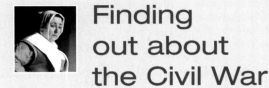

Finding out about the Civil War

Add a section to your diary about the Levellers. You could start your entry with one of these phrases:

- I have heard of these Levellers who believe...
- Yesterday I spoke to a Leveller who wore a green ribbon...
- Some Leveller ideas make sense to me...

Diary check

It is time to see how much you have learned about the Civil War and how well your diary has worked. Use the following checklist as you read through your finished diary.

Have you got:

- Paragraphs written in past, present and future tenses?

- Would someone reading your diary know it was meant to be set during the Civil War?

- Would someone reading your diary know which side you were on?

- Would someone reading your diary learn something about the thoughts and feelings of an ordinary soldier at that time?

Writing your guide

You are now ready to write your guide for Civil War re-enactors.

Most Civil War re-enactors take their hobby very seriously. They sometimes know as much about the detail of the period as many historians and teachers. They spend their time looking at the evidence from the seventeenth century and arguing over details about how things really were. However a few do not, as this extract from a re-enactors website shows:

> 'At worst it [re-enactment] can substitute pantomime for a genuine image of the past. At one end there will be someone who looks as though they really live in their outfit and is a mine of fascinating information on the period. They are probably wearing hand-stitched under-breeches (underwear) – not because they expect to show them to anyone, but because THEY know they have them on. At the other end is the re-enactor who will be hard-pressed to tell you when the Civil War actually started. They are probably wearing a big floppy hat covered in feathers, a black shirt, modern desert boots and a nineteenth century pewter tankard hanging from their belt!'

You should include the following in your guide:

- A short paragraph about the causes of the war

- Information about what fighting in a battle was like (including the different sorts of soldiers and weapons)

- Information about what different people would have worn (you might want to illustrate this section)

- Maps or illustrations to explain your text.

Use ICT software such as Publisher for this task if you can.

1642	1650	1660

1642	1646	1648	Dec 1648	Jan 1649	1649–1653
The First Civil War begins	Charles I surrenders to the Scots	The Second Civil War. Parliament wins	The 'Rump' Parliament puts Charles on trial for treason	Charles I is executed	England becomes a Commonwealth, run by the Rump Parliament

'A cruel necessity': why was the king executed?

SOURCE A

Charles I's execution, painted by an eyewitness

SOURCE B

January 30 1649

The king was brought from St James walking on foot through the Park, with colours flying, drums beating... to the gallery in Whitehall...

...about 12 at noon he drank a glass of claret wine and ate a piece of bread. From there he was accompanied through the Banqueting House, next to which the Scaffold was erected... The scaffold was hung round with black and the floor covered with black, and the axe and block laid in the middle of the Scaffold. The king, making a pause upon the scaffold, looked very earnestly at the block and asked if there was no higher.

The king, stooping down, laid his neck upon the block, and after very little pause, stretching forth his hands, the executioner at one blow severed his head from his body.

From The Intelligencer, *a contemporary newspaper*

ACTIVITIES

1. What impression does Source B give you about how King Charles I behaved at his execution?

2. Use both sources to write a list of adjectives. They should describe the emotions of people watching the execution – for example, 'horrified', 'distressed'...

3. Why might people watching the execution have different reactions to seeing the king die?

April 1653	July 1653	Dec 1653–1659	1657	1658	1660
Cromwell dismisses the Rump Parliament	Cromwell creates the Barebones Parliament	Cromwell becomes Lord Protector. The Protectorate is created	Cromwell refuses the Crown	Cromwell dies. His son, Richard, becomes Lord Protector	The monarchy is restored. Charles II becomes king

Link 6

> When the Civil War began many people assumed that Charles would win. They certainly never dreamt their king would end up on the scaffold.

In 1646 Charles surrendered to the Scots. They promptly handed him over to Parliament. Its leaders now faced a difficult problem: what to do with the captured King?

I think we should negotiate a peace with Charles. He is still the King, after all! If we let the army take control, there will be chaos!

All I need to do is play my enemies off against each other. Then the country will realise that that they need a king and come back to me.

Why should we negotiate with the King? The fact that we beat him in battle clearly shows God is on our side! We need to limit the power of the monarchy.

The King will need our support if he is ever to regain his power. But we want him to agree to make the English church like the Scottish **Presbyterian** one!

Charles rejected all peace offers. Despite promising not to, he escaped, but was quickly recaptured. Still he continued to plot. He made a secret agreement with the Scots and in 1648 they invaded. At the same time there were royalist uprisings across England. The Second Civil War had begun.

For many radicals in the army, this was the final straw. To them, the war proved that Charles was 'a man of blood' – there could never be peace whilst he was alive. In December 1648 army soldiers stopped moderate MPs entering Parliament. The remaining 'Rump' of 50 radical MPs immediately decided to put Charles on trial. He was charged with high treason. After a week long trial he was found guilty and three days later was executed.

ACTIVITIES

1. Write speech bubbles for two people who might have different ideas:

   a) A soldier who fought for King Charles

   b) A woman whose home was destroyed by the King's soldiers

2. Which of the characters is the most **radical**? Why do you think this?

3. Which of the characters is the most moderate? Explain your view.

4. List the reasons why you think Charles I was executed.

NEW WORDS

Presbyterian
the Protestant Church in Scotland. It was run differently to the English Church.

Radical
extreme

From Republic to Restoration

Oliver Cromwell 1599–1658

Cromwell was not born into a very rich or important family. He was a farmer and then MP for Cambridge. Cromwell was very religious. Like many supporters on Parliament's side in the Civil War he was a Puritan. Cromwell believed he was serving God. If he had a difficult decision to make, he often waited for a sign from God before choosing what to do.

Cromwell helped to form Parliament's New Model Army. This was a well trained and disciplined force that helped Parliament win the war.

The Commonwealth

The Rump Parliament established a Council of State to govern the country. The army, led by Oliver Cromwell, wanted the Rump to reform the government and the Church. But by 1653 the army was frustrated at the lack of progress. Many MPs in the Rump were corrupt, and they refused to hold elections for a new Parliament. On 20 April 1653 Cromwell led a group of musketeers into the House of Commons. After listening to the debate for a while, he stood up.

'You have sat here too long for the good you do. In the name of God, go!'

Cromwell dissolving Parliament

Look back

Do you remember the problems Charles I had with Parliament? When he took soldiers into Parliament in 1642, it sparked the Civil War. Now Cromwell was forced to do the same thing.

The Barebones Parliament

Cromwell replaced the Rump with an assembly, nicknamed the Barebones Parliament. Its members were chosen by the army. Cromwell hoped they would be easier to control than the Rump Parliament. But after months of squabbling, moderate members of the assembly walked out. Again, Cromwell had to send soldiers to disband the assembly. Now what would happen?

The Protectorate

Desperate to restore order, army officers drew up their own **constitution** called the Instrument of Government. Cromwell was made Lord Protector for life. He would share power with a Council of State and Parliament. In 1655 Cromwell established military districts across the country. Cromwell, the champion of Parliament in the 1640s, had established a military dictatorship.

In 1657 Parliament offered Cromwell the crown. For two months he agonised over the decision. What would God want him to do? Finally, in May that year, he gave his answer to Parliament.

Cromwell refused the crown. But to many people he seemed to be king in all but name.

The Restoration

Cromwell ruled as Lord Protector until his death in 1658. His heir, Richard, lacked his father's leadership skills and toughness and did not have the support of the army. Within months, Parliament and the army were arguing and Richard had resigned. But soon even the army were quarrelling about what to do next!

Charles I's son was also called Charles. He was in exile in Europe and seized the opportunity to return to England. He offered to settle all his differences with Parliament. When a new Parliament reassembled in April 1660, they declared Charles king. In May 1660 he triumphantly entered London. Britain was ruled by a king once more.

ACTIVITIES

Write sentences to explain the following terms:

Rump

Commonwealth

Barebones

Protectorate

Military dictatorship

Cromwell was addressed as 'Your Highness'.

The ceremony to make him Lord Protector looked a lot like a king's coronation.

He also had the right to nominate his successor, and chose his son, Richard!

He appointed members of an Upper House of Parliament.

He was made head of state for life.

He used the Banqueting House, where Charles I was executed, as his official residence.

ACTIVITIES

1. Here is a list of statements about events after Charles I's execution. Which statements do you agree with? Copy out your choices in chronological order.
   a) Charles should not have agreed to return without the same powers as his father.
   b) Cromwell should have agreed to become king.
   c) Cromwell should not have named his son as successor.
   d) Cromwell should not have behaved like a king.
   e) Parliament should not have asked Cromwell to become king.
   f) Cromwell was wrong to dismiss the Rump.

2. Why do you think Cromwell was invited to become king?

3. Do you think it was inevitable that the monarchy would be restored?

NEW WORDS

Commonwealth
a nation governed by the people

Constitution
a document establishing the principles of how a country should be governed

1633	1640	1650	1660	1670

1633	1660	1660	1665	1666
Pepys is born	The Restoration: Charles II becomes king	Pepys starts writing his diary	The Great Plague	The Great Fire of London

1660 – 1669

London in the 1660s: What can we learn from Samuel Pepys's diary?

Who was Samuel Pepys?

Samuel Pepys was born in London. He went to school there, before going to study at Cambridge. Pepys (pronounced 'peeps') was the son of a tailor. He went on to become Secretary to the **Admiralty**.

Though he became an important and wealthy man, Pepys is most famous for the diary he kept between 1660 and 1669. The diary was written in a kind of shorthand code and took up six volumes. At 1,250,000 words it is a huge piece of evidence about England at that time.

Samuel Pepys wrote about daily events in his life and his interest in collecting books, playing music and going to the theatre. Pepys only stopped keeping the diary when his wife died of fever and his eyesight became poor. Many entries in the diary finish with the words, 'And so to bed.'

NEW WORDS

Admiralty
  the organisation in charge of the navy

London in the seventeenth century

1680　　　　　1690　　　　　1700 1703

1669
Pepys finishes
keeping his
diary

1703
Death of Pepys

*Samuel Pepys
1633–1703*

Finding out about Pepys's London

In this unit you are going to design a website travel guide for visitors to Samuel Pepys's London. The designs for the best websites on the Internet often start life on paper. It's similar to the way films and TV programmes are storyboarded before filming starts (see *History First 1066–1500*, page 107). So, even if you have access to a computer, sketch out your ideas on paper first.

As you work through the unit, note down any information you want to include and make rough sketches of each page. You will need these when you design your site at the end.

1 First of all you need a home page for your website. What will the name of your website be? It needs to tell visitors to the website what the site is all about, as well as being appealing!

2 Decide on a graphic for your home page. Will it be a street scene, map or picture of Pepys?

3 Write a paragraph briefly telling your audience what your website is about. You may wish to look through the next few pages of this unit to get some extra ideas.

As you write each section of your website think about the following:

- **What details are going to be on each page**. It is important not to crowd your website with too much information, so you will need to select your information carefully.

- **How to show your information clearly**. Good websites don't have long pages of text. You might want to use bullet points or different headings to make your text easier to read.

- **How to make your web pages interesting**. What graphics or pictures could you include to liven up the pages? You could research different websites to see how they are designed.

The weather

The diary has details about the weather at the time. Pepys often refers to cold frosty days. And we know that the River Thames was sometimes frozen over so thickly that fairs were held on the ice. However, the summers were warmer, as this extract suggests.

11 September 1661

To Dr. Williams, who did carry me into his garden, where he hath **abundance** of grapes; and did show me how a dog that he hath do kill all the cats that come thither to kill his pigeons; and he tells me that he do believe that he hath killed above 100 cats.

Pepys's diary shows that some dangers of living in London stemmed from natural causes.

18 February 1662

Walking in the streets, which were every where full of bricks and tiles flung down by the extraordinary wind the last night that it was dangerous to go out of doors; and hearing how several persons had been killed to-day by the fall of things in the streets, and that one Lady Sanderson, a person of quality in Covent Garden, was killed by the fall of the house, in her bed, last night.

ACTIVITIES

1. What clue does Source A give us about the climate at that time?

2. What does Pepys mean by a 'person of quality' in Source B?

A frost fair on the Thames

Travel

Pepys's diary gives us an idea of what travel around London was like that no picture source can manage.

Pepys sometimes travelled by coach, but often walked around the city. Like most Londoners, if he was near the River Thames, he usually travelled by boat.

We know that travel was not always safe. The men who ran the river boats were a particularly tough lot.

NEW WORDS

Abundance
plenty

ACTIVITIES

1. Explain why it might have been 'extraordinary dark' in Source C.

2. Describe the incident in Source E in your own words.

There were about 40,000 Thames watermen, who rowed travellers across the Thames

Finding out about Pepys's London

1. Use Sources A–E to write down at least five adjectives that you think describe life in London at that time. Try to use them when you are writing the different pages for your website.

2. You now need to add a new page to your website. It will need to include information on the weather; travelling and staying safe in the city.

   - Think of what headings you will use for each section.

   - Decide what information you will need to include under each heading. Make sure you use some quotes from Pepys's diary.

   - Think about how to organise your information.

   - What pictures or graphics could you use? For example, do you need a map to show people places to visit, and where to avoid?

   - Design a link or icon representing each section, to go on the home page. You will need to add an icon and a label each time you design a new page.

Entertainment

Pepys liked to enjoy himself, and there can be few forms of entertainment available in London that are not mentioned in the diary. **Bear-baiting** was still going on and Pepys described it as a 'very rude and nasty pleasure'. With the restoration of Charles II, theatres re-opened and, unlike in Shakespeare's day, the women's parts were played by women. Here are some diary extracts that show what entertainment was available and what Pepys thought of them.

SOURCE A

2 December 1661

By and by called on by Mr. Sanchy and his mistress, and with them by coach to the Opera, to see "The Mad Lover", but not much pleased with the play.

SOURCE B

16 August 1662

So to the Swan, in Old Fish Street and after dinner comes in a juggler, which showed us very pretty tricks.

SOURCE C

29 September 1662

Then to the King's Theatre, where we saw "Midsummer's Night's Dream", which I had never seen before, nor shall ever again, for it is the most insipid ridiculous play that ever I saw in my life. I saw, I confess, some good dancing and some handsome women, which was all my pleasure.

A group of comic actors

A dancing bear

SOURCE D

1 June 1663

To the New Theatre and here I came and saw the first prize I ever saw in my life: and it was between one Mathews and one Westwicke, who was soundly cut several times both in the head and legs, that he was all over blood. They fought at eight weapons, three **bouts** at each weapon. It was very well worth seeing.

SOURCE E

27 November 1662

Went to see the coming by of the Russian Ambassador. I could not see the Ambassador in his coach; but his attendants in their habits and fur caps very handsome, comely men, and most of them with hawks upon their fists to present to the King. But Lord! To see the absurd nature of Englishmen, that cannot **forbear** laughing and jeering at every thing that looks strange.

A conjuror performing magic tricks

An acrobat

Some forms of entertainment were very different from those of today.

SOURCE F

27 February 1663

After dinner I went along to see the body of a lusty fellow, a seaman, that was hanged for a robbery. I did touch the dead body with my bare hand: it felt cold, but methought it was a very unpleasant sight. But all the Doctors at table conclude, that there is no pain at all in hanging, for that it do stop the circulation of the blood; and so stops all sense and motion in an instant.

Executions were public events. They were intended to send a warning to people.

SOURCE G

13 October 1660

I went out to Charing Cross to see Major-General Harrison hanged, drawn, and quartered he looking as cheerfully as any man could do in that condition. He was cut down and his head and his heart shown to the people, at which there was great shouts of joy.

ACTIVITIES

1. List the different forms of entertainment described by Pepys.

2. Which of these entertainments did Pepys enjoy most? Write down any phrases from the diary that helped you choose.

3. Which of the entertainments did Pepys enjoy least? Write down any phrases from the diary that helped you choose.

NEW WORDS

Bear-baiting
  dogs attacking a chained bear
Bouts
  rounds
Forbear
  stop themselves

Finding out about Pepys's London

You now need to add another page to your website.

1. Think of the heading you will use for this section.

2. Make notes and rough sketches for the web page giving advice about entertainment in the city. Use your answers to activities 1–3 to help you.

3. Think about how to organise your information.

Design a link or icon representing this section to go on your home page. Don't forget to design a link back to your home page.

Food and drink

Pepys liked to describe in detail what he had eaten. Sometimes it was meals for special occasions like this celebration dinner.

SOURCE A

4 April 1663

Very merry at dinner. We had a fricassee of rabbits and chickens, a leg of mutton boiled, three carps in a dish, a great dish of a side of lamb, a dish of roasted pigeons, a dish of four lobsters, three tarts, a lamprey pie (a most rare pie), a dish of anchovies, good wine of several sorts, and all things mighty noble and to my great content.

Even everyday meals are recorded in the diary.

SOURCE B

7 Sept 1663

Black Spread Eagle in Bride Lane, and there had a chop of veal and some bread, cheese, and beer, cost me a shilling [5p] to my dinner.

Sometimes we get information about what was new or unusual.

SOURCE C

1 December 1661

We this day cut a brave collar of brawn and also opened the glass of gherkins which are rare things.

Most men drank beer every day or wine if they were better off. In coffee houses men could read the paper or chat together. The coffee was usually served in glasses and was black and sweet. Tea was mainly a drink for the rich.

SOURCE D

28 September 1660

I did send for a cup of tea (a China drink) of which I had never drunk before.

A London coffee house in the seventeenth century

Chocolate was first drunk in England about 1652. In this extract Pepys gives us a clue about how it was seen by the people at the time.

SOURCE E

24 April 1661

Waked in the morning with my head in a sad taking through the last night's drink, rose and went out with Mr. Creed to drink our morning draught, which he did give me in chocolate to settle my stomach.

ACTIVITIES

1. Why might gherkins (Source C) have been 'rare things' at that time?

2. Suggest a reason why Pepys might think drinking chocolate (Source E) was good for a hangover.

3. Copy and complete this table about food mentioned by Pepys, using Sources A–E.

Food you have eaten	Food you have not eaten, but you think is eaten in Britain today	Food you think is not eaten in Britain today

NEW WORDS

Anchovies
small saltwater fish

Brawn
preserved meat from a pig's or calf's head

Carps
freshwater fish

Draught
drink of medicine

Fricassee
stewed or fried meat in a thick sauce

Gherkins
small pickled cucumbers

Lamprey
an eel-like fish

Poultice
cloth and medicine, usually applied to
a sore or growth

Medical treatment

Pepys suffered from various illnesses while he was keeping his diary, including failing eyesight. The diary gives us valuable evidence about medical treatments at the time. Here is a treatment he used for a boil, which seemed to work.

SOURCE F

18 October 1661

A poultice of a good handful of bran with half a pint of vinegar and a pint of water boiled till it be thick, and then a spoonful of honey put to it and so spread in a cloth and laid to it.

Bleeding a patient was a very common treatment. Usually a small cut was made in a vein in the arm and the blood allowed to drain out. It was believed that too much blood in the body was harmful.

SOURCE G

14 July 1668

This morning I was let blood, and did bleed about fourteen ounces, towards curing my eyes.

 **ACTIVITY**

What can you work out from Sources F and G about how good medical treatment was at that time?

....

But Pepys was lucky these illnesses were not life threatening ... unlike the Great Plague.

Finding out about Pepys's London

The next page of your website will be your advice about what to eat and drink in London, and where visitors can eat out.

1 Think of a heading for the new page.

2 Select your information, including quotes from Pepys's diary and make some rough sketches.

3 Think about how to organise your information.

A doctor bleeding a patient

Finding out about Pepys's London

Make notes for a new section of your web guide giving advice about what to do in case of illness. You will be adding to this on pages 108–109.

107

The Great Plague

Pepys's diary gives us some of the most detailed evidence available about the Great Plague of 1665.

Plague had never completely disappeared from England since the Black Death in the Middle Ages. There were outbreaks every few years, usually lasting through the summer and dying away as colder weather came. 1665 was the year of the last major outbreak of plague in England. Perhaps one in five people in London died from the disease. No one knew that it was spread by fleas living on black rats. The rats, in turn, lived on the filth in London's streets. Pepys's diary not only provides details of what happened, it also gives us a human interpretation of events. It describes how families affected by plague could be shut up in their homes.

Look back

What do you remember about the plague? What were the symptoms? Look back at pages 85–89 in *History First 1066–1500* to remind yourself.

ACTIVITY

Write two or three sentences to describe what you think is happening in each scene shown in Source A.

NEW WORDS

- **Apothecary**
  chemist
- **Physician**
  trained doctor

SOURCE A

Pictures from a leaflet about the plague published in 1666

SOURCE B

The Diseases and Casualties this Week.

Disease	Number	Disease	Number
Abortive	6	Kingsevil	10
Aged	54	Lethargy	1
Apoplexie	1	Murthered at Stepney	1
Bedridden	1	Palsie	2
Cancer	2	Plague	3880
Childbed	23	Plurisie	1
Chrisomes	15	Quinsie	6
Collick		Rickets	23
Consumption	174	Rising of the Lights	19
Convulsion	88	Rupture	2
Dropsie	40	Sciatica	1
Drowned two, one at St.Kath. Tower, and one at Lambeth	2	Scowring	13
		Scurvy	1
		Sore legge	1
Feaver	353	Spotted Feaver and Purples	190
Fistula	1	Starved at Nurse	1
Flox and Small-pox	10	Stilborn	8
Flux	2	Stone	2
Found dead in the Street at St.Bartholomew the Less	1	Stopping of the stomach	16
		Strangury	1
Frighted	1	Suddenly	1
Gangrene	1	Surfeit	87
Gowt	1	Teeth	113
Grief	1	Thrush	3
Griping in the Guts	74	Tissick	6
Jaundies	3	Ulcer	2
Imposthume	18	Vomiting	7
Infants	21	Winde	8
Killed by a fall down stairs at St. Thomas Apostle	1	Wormes	18

Christned { Males — 83 Females — 83 In all — 166 }   Buried { Males — 2656 Females — 2663 In all — 5319 }   Plague — 3880

Increased in the Burials this Week — 1289
Parishes clear of the Plague — 34   Parishes Infected — 96

The Assize of Bread set forth by Order of the Lord Maior and Court of Aldermen,
A penny Wheaten Loaf to contain Nine Ounces and a half, and three half-penny White Loaves the like weight.

A Bill of Mortality for one week during the Great Plague. This was a list of how people were thought to have died

ACTIVITIES

1. Look at Source B. List the five most frequent causes of death and numbers who died.

2. List any causes of death that you do not recognise.

3. What is the difference between the number of people buried and the number of people christened (born)?

4. Suggest a reason why details about bread are shown on this sheet.

The following extracts were recorded by Pepys from June to October 1665...

SOURCE C

7 June 1665

It being the hottest day that ever I felt in my life. This day I did in Drury Lane see two or three houses marked with a red cross upon the doors, and 'Lord have mercy upon us' writ there—which was a sad sight to me being the first of that kind that I ever saw.

SOURCE D

3 September 1665

Up, and put on my silk suit but I dare not wear my new wig because the plague was in Westminster when I bought it. And I wonder what will be the fashion after the plague is done, for nobody will dare to buy any hair for fear of the infection—that it had been cut off the heads of people dead of the plague.

SOURCE E

16 October 1665

But Lord, how empty the streets are, so many poor sick people in the streets, full of sores, and so many sad stories overheard as I walk, everybody talking of this dead, and that man sick, and so many in this place, and so many in that. And they tell me that in Westminster there is never a **physician**, and but one **apothecary** left, all being dead.

ACTIVITIES

1. Write down any phrases from the diary that provided evidence about the Great Plague that we could not get from another type of source.

2. Which of the three types of source do you think is most useful for finding out about the plague: the diary, the pictures or the Bill of Mortality? Why? Try to give some reasons for your choice.

Finding out about Pepys's London

1. Add to the notes you made giving advice about what to do in case of illness.

2. Choose a heading for your page.

3. Think about how to organise your information and make some rough sketches.

The Great Fire

*A painting made soon after the fire. The artist may have been an eyewitness.
The Tower is on the right, St Paul's in the centre and London Bridge on the left*

Many buildings were, at least partly, made of wood. Houses were packed close together and one of the only ways to stop a fire spreading was to tear down houses in the path of the flames or blow them up with gunpowder to make a fire break. There were no fire engines or fire brigades, in anything like the modern sense, to tackle a major blaze.

The Great Fire of 1666 seems to have started by accident in a baker's shop in Pudding Lane. The dry weather and a strong wind meant it spread rapidly.

SOURCE A

2 September 1666

Jane called up about three in the morning, to tell us of a great fire they saw in the City. By and by Jane comes and tells me that she hears that above 300 houses have been burned down tonight by the fire we saw, and that it is now burning down all Fish Street, by London Bridge.

Pepys realised the danger of the fire. He went to tell King Charles II, who ordered that houses should be pulled down in front of the advancing flames. Pepys was sent to tell the Lord Mayor of London what to do.

SOURCE B

2 September 1666

At last I met my Lord Mayor in Canning Street. To the King's message he cried, like a fainting woman, 'Lord, what can I do? I am spent: people will not obey me. I have been pulling down houses, but the fire overtakes us faster than we can do it.'

The scale of the fire and how it affected individuals can be seen in Pepys's diary.

SOURCE C

2 September 1666

We staid till, it being darkish, we saw the fire as only one entire arch of fire from this to the other side the bridge, and in a bow up the hill for an arch of above a mile long: it made me weep to see it. The churches, houses, and all on fire and flaming at once; and a horrid noise the flames made, and the cracking of houses at their ruins.

SOURCE D

28 February 1667

I did within these six days see smoke still remaining of the late fire in the City; and it is strange to think how I cannot sleep a-night without great terrors of fire.

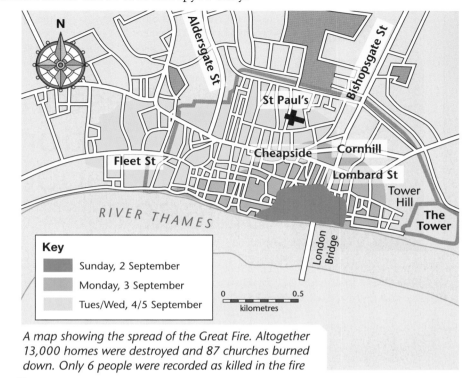

Key
- Sunday, 2 September
- Monday, 3 September
- Tues/Wed, 4/5 September

0   0.5
kilometres

A map showing the spread of the Great Fire. Altogether 13,000 homes were destroyed and 87 churches burned down. Only 6 people were recorded as killed in the fire

👁 ACTIVITIES

1 Suggest some reasons why few people died in the fire.

2 Use the map to work out which way the wind was blowing.

3 Explain why people might not obey the Lord Mayor (Source B).

4 Use Sources A–C and the painting opposite to help you write your own diary entry for 2 September 1666.

Finding out about Pepys's London

1 Make notes and sketches for a web page about the Great Fire either based on the map or the painting.

2 On your web page you should have a checklist for tourists visiting London after the Great Fire. It could include things to look out for, such as new buildings.

You may need to do some research on how the Great Fire changed London.

Now it's time to produce the final design for your website.

You will need to use your notes to write the text for each page of your site. Make sure that you have similar amounts of information on each page. You also need to check that you are not repeating information on different pages.

If you are unhappy with the quotes from Pepys's diary that you have chosen you can change them. An indexed version of much of Pepys's diary can be found on the Internet at www.pepysdiary.com. (The whole diary can be downloaded from the Project Gutenberg site www.gutenberg.org.)

Review your website design. Have you included all the graphics and pictures you need? Make sure you have notes about font, point sizes and colour schemes.

1660	1670	1680	1688

1660	1668	1678		
Monarchy is restored. Charles II becomes King	Charles's brother and heir, James becomes a Catholic	Catholics are no longer allowed to sit in the House of Lords	Suspected Catholic plot to kill Charles II	Death of Edmund Godfrey

From Restoration to Revolution: what was glorious about the events of 1688?

In 1688 there was another revolution. This is known as the Glorious Revolution. Unlike the revolution of the 1640s, this one was short and almost completely peaceful.

The mysterious death of Edmund Godfrey

On the afternoon of 17 October 1678 two men walked out of the rain into an inn near London. They told the landlord they had just seen a gentleman's cane and a **scabbard** lying beside a deep ditch. They described the ditch as covered with brambles. When the rain stopped, a group went to investigate. They found the body of a man lying face downwards, with his feet caught up in the brambles. A sword was sticking through his body. The dead man was recognised as Sir Edmund Godfrey. He had been missing for five days.

Two surgeons held a post-mortem on the corpse. They found that Godfrey had died two or three days before his body was found. His chest was bruised as if he had been beaten or kicked. He had been strangled by a cloth and his neck was broken. He had two stab wounds. The lack of blood showed that both of these wounds had happened after he died.

The scene of the crime

The area around the ditch was trampled down by the men who found the body, but the following points were noted:

- No blood was found around the ditch.
- The sword found sticking in the body was Godfrey's own.
- Godfrey's shoes were quite clean.
- A large amount of money was found on Godfrey's body.
- The body had not been in the ditch two days earlier. This was known because a local man had hunted with his dogs there.

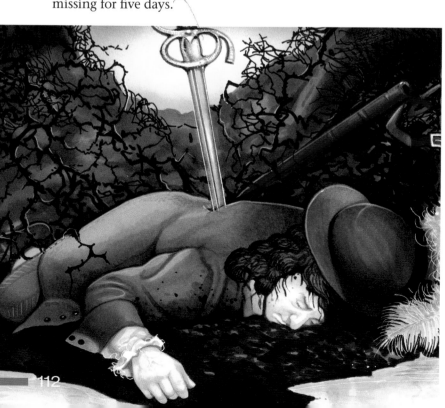

Who was Edmund Godfrey?

Edmund Godfrey was a merchant. He was also the **Justice of the Peace (JP)** for the City of Westminster. Godfrey took his work as a JP seriously. He was often seen around the city at odd times of the day or night looking for criminals. Godfrey was not afraid to take on important men if necessary. He even tried to have the king's physician arrested for debt. We also know that Godfrey was friendly to Catholics and had made business deals with them. He was not in favour of persecuting any religious groups.

Godfrey was sometimes moody. He was believed to have been suffering from depression at the time of his death. Shortly before he disappeared, Godfrey said that he thought he was in danger.

In September 1678 a man named Titus Oates twice went to Godfrey's home and gave him sworn details of a Catholic plot to kill the King. Oates said that once Charles II was dead, his brother James would become king and thousands of Protestants would be **massacred**. It seems that Godfrey thought that Oates was lying about the plot.

Sir Edmund Godfrey

ACTIVITIES

1. Using all the information on pages 112 and 113, make a list of anything that you find suspicious about Sir Edmund Godfrey's death.

2. Now put your list in order, with the most suspicious point first. You can do this by rewriting the list or by numbering it.

NEW WORDS

Justice of the Peace (JP)
civil judge or magistrate

Massacred
killed in large numbers

Scabbard
sword-holder

Finding out about 1688

In this unit you are going to find out why there was another revolution in 1688 and what Titus Oates and Sir Edmund Godfrey have to do with all this! Your final activity will be to create a presentation explaining the causes of the Glorious Revolution.

As you work through the unit you will complete a table to help you decide what the causes of the Revolution were, and how important each cause was.

1. Copy out the table opposite. Remember to leave lots of space so you can go back and add to your entries.

Cause of Revolution	Why this is a cause	How important is this cause?
Edmund Godfrey's murder		

2. Re-read the story of Edmund Godfrey's murder. Can you find anything in the story that links the events to the revolution of 1688? Don't worry if you can't – you will have a chance to come back to it later!

Who were the **suspects?**

The servants?

Three men, Robert Green, Lawrence Hill and Henry Berry, were arrested and eventually executed for the murder of Sir Edmund Godfrey. They were probably innocent. The men were servants at the house where Sir Edmund was thought to have been killed. The only evidence against them came from paid informers.

Godfrey's enemies?

It is likely that Sir Edmund made enemies through his work as a JP. One of them could have murdered him to get revenge, or for some other reason. Some people have suggested that his death was the result of a simple mugging.

Suicide?

Another theory was that Sir Edmund had committed suicide but afterwards someone had tried to make the death look like murder. Perhaps they wanted an excuse to try to blame the Catholics. Perhaps it was his family who covered up a suicide. At that time everything owned by someone who killed themselves was taken by the king. Sir Edmund's family would lose everything.

Titus Oates?

One person who is often named as the real murderer is Titus Oates. He was the man who had brought news of the Catholic plot to Sir Edmund. Perhaps he killed him to make his story of a plot seem more real.

Sir Edmund Godfrey became a hero. Pamphlets were published discussing the murder and thousands of people turned out for his funeral.

Even the most important people in the country were not safe from being linked to the murder. Years later King Charles's brother James, a Catholic, was named as being involved in Sir Edmund's death.

The Catholics?

At the time many people believed that Catholics were behind the murder. It was seen as part of the wider plot against the king described by Titus Oates. Oates encouraged this situation, to stir up further fear and hatred of Catholics.

Who was Titus Oates?

For a while, Titus Oates was one of the most popular men in England. The son of a Protestant preacher, Oates was expelled from school. He became a vicar in the Church of England but was dismissed twice for drunkenness, theft and **lewd** behaviour. He then took a post as a naval chaplain but was quickly dismissed from that too.

Disgraced, Oates fled to Europe and temporarily joined the Catholic Jesuit Order. He claimed he had pretended to become a Catholic so he could learn their secrets. When Oates was expelled from the Order he returned to England and became friends with an extreme anti-Catholic preacher, Israel Tonge. Tonge had already made claims about Catholic plots against the King.

Titus Oates (1649–1705)

NEW WORDS

Lewd
crude and offensive

ACTIVITY

We do not know who was responsible for Sir Edmund Godfrey's death. What do you think happened?

1. Pick the theory you think is most likely to be correct. Give some reasons for your choice.

or

2. Write your own theory about how, and why, Sir Edmund Godfrey died.

Finding out about 1688

1. Re-read the story of the murder on pages 112–114. Use the information to add more details to the entry in your table about how Sir Edmund Godfrey's murder might be linked to the Revolution in 1688.

2. How important do you now think Godfrey's murder was?

Popish **plots**

You may have realised there is a strong theme in many of the units of this book. That theme is the religious tensions in England in the sixteenth and seventeenth centuries.

By the 1670s, the number of Catholics in different parts of England varied. In some parts of the country, mainly in the west, Catholics made up as much as 20% of the population. In most places they were treated with deep suspicion. Sometimes that suspicion could turn to fear and hatred.

In an atmosphere of fear, stories and rumours about 'popish plots' seemed very real. In 1666 many people blamed the Catholics for starting the Fire of London.

Look back

Look back to Unit 5: Gunpowder, treason... and plot. How did the plot affect attitudes towards Catholics?

In the late summer of 1678, Charles II heard about the plot by Catholic conspirators to kill him. Titus Oates was brought before the Privy Council. He changed his story so many times that today historians say he was lying. But this was not what many people thought in 1678. The King did nothing. Some people suspected that this was because Charles was sympathetic to the Catholic religion. He is quoted as saying that Catholicism was 'the only religion fit for a gentleman'.

From the autumn of 1678, Sir Edmund Godfrey's murder started a series of scares and rumours that put the country on edge for the next three years. There were wild stories about Catholic troops preparing to overrun the country, of cellars full of swords and of the French army landing on the south coast of England.

Between 1678 and 1681 Parliament investigated the 'popish plot'. Thirty-five people were executed, despite the lack of real evidence. But it didn't stop there. The popish plots would have terrible consequences for the monarchy itself. Why?

One way that events were recorded in the seventeenth century was on playing cards

ACTIVITY

Why do you think people believed the rumours about popish plots?

Finding out about 1688

1. Re-read the story of Edmund Godfrey's murder on pages 112–113. Think about what the information on the Popish plots adds to your understanding of the story:
   - What were the effects of Edmund Godfrey's murder?

2. Go back to the entry in your table. Add any extra information to the 'Why this is a cause' column.

3. Do you still agree with what you have written in the 'How important is this cause' column?

Restoration and succession

In 1660 the monarchy was restored. But when Charles II returned to England, many MPs were anxious. They thought that he might try to bring back his father's ideas about 'the Divine Right of Kings'. Charles I believed the king's power and authority were a direct gift from God. This meant the king was above the control of Parliament. MPs did not want an **absolute monarchy**. On the other hand, many people thought Parliament had gone too far in the 1640s and wanted to ensure it did not have so much power.

In the 1660s the king could still call and **dissolve** Parliament as he wished. He could **veto** any Parliamentary legislation and appoint whom he wanted as an adviser. But the newly appointed monarch could not punish Parliament for its actions in the 1640s and 1650s. Far too many people had been involved. King and Parliament needed to find a compromise.

Charles II was a popular king on the whole, and was known as the Merry Monarch. He loved wine, women and gambling. He had a number of mistresses and 13 illegitimate children. But he had no children through his marriage to Catherine of Braganza, a Portuguese princess.

Then, in 1668 the king's brother and heir, James, publicly announced he had become a Catholic.

> With the King suspected of being a Catholic sympathiser and his brother openly Catholic, the succession to the throne became a big question.

Charles II

4 Add 'Popish plots' in the 'Cause of Revolution' column of your table.

Add any evidence you can find that the plots were a cause of the 1688 Revolution in the 'Why this is a cause' column. Here are some clues to help you:

- Why might people have been concerned about Charles II's reaction to the plots?
- What sort of atmosphere did the plots create in the country?

5 Decide how important you think the plots were as a cause of the Revolution, and add your answer to your table.

Finding out about 1688

1 Add two new rows to your table:
   Power of the monarch
   James's Catholic beliefs

2 For each one, add any evidence you can find about why it was a cause, and how important it was.

   Does the story of the Restoration and succession help to explain why Godfrey's murder and the Popish plots were causes of the Revolution?

3 Go back and add to or change your previous entries.

Who should be **king?**

At the same time as Parliament was investigating the popish plots, questions started to be asked about who should become king after Charles. Historians call this question of succession the 'exclusion crisis' simply because the main aim was to exclude James from the succession because he was a Catholic.

One Parliamentary group (known as the Whigs) wanted a law to be passed that would firmly exclude James. Charles was furious with Parliament and wanted it thrown out. The leader of the Whig group was the Earl of Shaftesbury. He'd fought for both Crown and Parliament and supported both Cromwell and Charles. Shaftsbury organised huge demonstrations and petitions in favour of exclusion.

Charles's supporters in Parliament were known as the Tories. They used people's memories of the 1640s and 1650s to frighten them away from the Exclusion Bill. Did people really want civil war again? The answer in the 1680s was NO! Charles got the support he needed and the Bill was lost. Shaftesbury plotted a revolt and was defeated. He fled the country and died in **exile**.

The contenders

James Stuart (1633–1701)

James was made Duke of York in 1644. He spent much of his youth in exile, and served in the French army. James became a Catholic in 1668. He married twice. His first wife, Anne Hyde, died in 1671 after bearing eight children. Only two of their children, Mary and Anne, survived into adulthood. James married again in 1673. His second wife, Mary of Modena, was a strict Catholic and was hated by the English public.

James, Duke of Monmouth (1649–1685)

James was the illegitimate son of Charles II and his mistress Lucy Walker. Later he was made Duke of Monmouth and claimed that his parents had been secretly married. However, Charles never named him as heir to the throne. Monmouth became a very successful army commander. He was popular, partly because he was a Protestant.

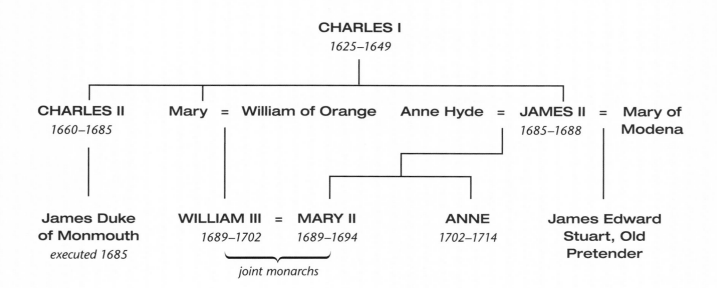

```
                        CHARLES I
                        1625–1649
                            |
    ┌───────────────┬───────────────────┬──────────────────────────┐
CHARLES II      Mary = William of Orange      Anne Hyde = JAMES II = Mary of
1660–1685                                               1685–1688   Modena
    |               |              ┌────────────┴──────┐              |
James Duke      WILLIAM III = MARY II              ANNE          James Edward
of Monmouth     1689–1702    1689–1694            1702–1714      Stuart, Old
executed 1685        └────────┬────────┘                        Pretender
                         joint monarchs
```

Mary (1662–1694) and William of Orange (1650–1702)

Mary was the eldest daughter of James II and Anne Hyde. In 1677 Mary married her cousin William III, Prince of Orange. They were both Protestants. During the exclusion crisis many people thought James II should step aside to make room for his daughter and her husband.

The crisis died away and by the end of 1682 the wild idea of popish plots seemed to be over. Titus Oates was imprisoned and flogged for calling the King's brother a traitor.

👁 ACTIVITIES

1. Look at the family tree for the Stuarts. Who is the most likely contender to the throne?

2. Who do you think might be the strongest contender?

NEW WORDS

Exile
being forced to live outside one's own country

Finding out about 1688

1. Use the information in this section and your answers to activities 1 and 2 to add to the information in your table under 'James's Catholic beliefs'.

2. Look back at the other rows in your table. Add any extra information to the 'Why this was a cause' column.

3. How important do you now think each cause was? If you have changed your mind, amend your answers in the 'How important is this cause' column.

The road to **revolution**

In 1681 Charles II dissolved Parliament and for the next four years of his reign he ruled without calling Parliament. When Charles died in 1685 the monarchy seemed to be in a strong position. It looked as though James II would be a popular choice for king. So, what happened? Look carefully at these cards, they tell some of the story of the years that led up to 1688.

E

the godly Maids of Taunton pr'senting their Colours upon their knees to y D. of M.

7
The Protestant Duke of Monmouth was the illegitimate son of Charles II. He landed with a force of just 82 men at Lyme Regis in June 1685. He wanted to replace James II as king. Within days he had over 1,000 supporters. When Monmouth reached Taunton he was greeted by cheering crowds. He was given a flag for his army by the women of the town.

2
In April 1688 seven bishops were arrested for refusing to support James II over the ending of anti-Catholic laws. They were put on trial but found not guilty. Londoners lit bonfires to celebrate the result of the trial.

A

The Army going over to y Prince of Orange.

4
James II sent Judge Jeffreys to the West Country to try those who took part in the Monmouth Rebellion of 1685. Over 300 were executed and 800 were sold as slaves to work in the West Indies.

G

Severall of y Rebells hang'd upon a Tree

1
Leading politicians asked William of Orange, James's Protestant son-in-law, for help. William landed on 5 November 1688 with a Dutch army. James II was allowed to escape to France. William drove peacefully into London while the church bells rang out in greeting. William and his wife Mary were crowned king and queen.

B

Conspirators waiting for y K. coming by Rumbole House

C

The Tryal of the Seaven Bishops

1 Copy and complete this table, matching the playing cards to the correct event, and sorting your answers into chronological order.

Chronological order	Card letter	Event number	Sentence summary of the event
1st			
2nd			
3rd			
4th			
5th			
6th			
7th			

2 Colour-code your table to show when the Catholics seem to be 'doing well' and when they seem to be 'doing badly'.

3 How did James go from being a popular king in 1685 to an exiled king in 1688?

3

In July 1685 Monmouth's army was defeated by the King's men at the Battle of Sedgemoor. Monmouth was captured and taken to London to be executed.

6

In 1683 there was a plot to assassinate King Charles and his brother as they were going home from the Newmarket races. The plan was to shoot them as they went along a narrow lane by Rye House in Hertfordshire. The Duke of Monmouth would then be made King. A fire at Newmarket forced the king to return home early and the plot failed. Most of those involved were arrested and executed. This event became known as the Rye House Plot.

F

QUEEN ♣

The Defeat of the Rebells
2000 Slayn & their Canon taken

Finding out about 1688

Add two new rows to your table:

Monmouth's rebellion
James's unpopularity

1 Use the information in this section and your answers to activity 3 to help you decide why each of these factors was a cause of the Revolution, and how important they were. Add your answers to the table.

2 Use the information on the spread to add to your previous entries in your table. Revise your answers to how important each cause was if you have changed your opinion.

5

Titus Oates' story of a 'popish plot' led to the arrest and execution of 35 people. 1679 became a time of panic and rumour. Harsh anti-Catholic laws were used. Priests were arrested and Catholic books were burned.

A Glorious Revolution?

You have seen how the Protestant William of Orange landed in England with a Dutch army. James II was forced flee abroad. What is surprising is that this change of monarch turned out to be peaceful. There were no big battles or executions and the event became known as the 'Glorious Revolution'. So why did this 'revolution' happen, and why was it almost completely peaceful?

While James II was king he became unpopular. He gave important jobs in the army, navy and government to Catholics. He also **suspended** some laws without Parliament's agreement. Despite this, he might have remained king, particularly as both his daughters were brought up as Protestants. But when James's wife gave birth to a son, many Protestants feared that England might become Catholic again forever. This led leading Protestants to ask William of Orange to come and defend their religion.

Probably fewer than 100 men were killed in the skirmishes of 1688. This was mainly because many of James's soldiers deserted or refused to obey their Catholic officers. Even some leaders in his army changed sides. Also William was clever enough to allow James to escape to France. Everyone could remember what happened to Charles I after his arrest. With James fleeing in this way, Parliament could claim the throne was free to give to William and his wife, Mary. In the following year Parliament passed a Bill of Rights. This made certain there could never be a Catholic monarch in England again.

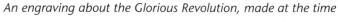

An engraving about the Glorious Revolution, made at the time

EXTENSION ACTIVITY

Do you think that the English monarchy was secure after 1688? Write a paragraph explaining your reasons for your answer. You may wish to do some research into events over the next 100 years to extend your answer.

NEW WORDS

Censored
controlled by the government

Suspended
stopped

Finding out about 1688

You are now ready to create a presentation giving your interpretation of the events that led to the Glorious Revolution.

One way that events were recorded in the seventeenth century was on playing cards. These were printed soon after something important happened. The cards helped to tell people what was going on as newspapers were **censored**. You will use the idea of playing cards to present your interpretation.

Check you have seven causes in your table:

Edmund Godfrey's murder
Power of the monarch
Popish plots
James's Catholic beliefs
Monmouth's rebellion
James's unpopularity
James's heir

1. Design one playing card to represent each cause. Think carefully about what information you want to show on your cards. Which particular part of the story will you show?

2. For each card, write a caption of no more than 50 words summing up why it was a cause of the Revolution in 1688.

3. Use the information in your table and your cards and captions to help you organise your presentation. You will need to think about:

   - **The importance of each cause.** Which cause do you think was most important? Which cause do you think was least important? Remember to explain why you think this!

   - **The order you will present the causes in.** Will you organise your presentation chronologically? Will you organise it by order of importance? Or will you organise it by theme, e.g. political and religious causes?

   - **How to present your points clearly.** Use numbered lists and bullet points to make your information easier for your audience to understand.

4. How will you present your information? Can you use an ICT package such as PowerPoint?

Finding out about 1688

1. Add more details to the row in your table on James's unpopularity.

2. Add a new row for the cause 'James's heir'. Use the information on this page to fill in the sections on 'Why this is a cause' and 'How important is this cause?'.

Renaissance **inventions**

The fifteenth and sixteenth centuries in Europe are known as the Renaissance. This was a time when there was a great interest in classical civilisations like the Greeks and the Romans, in learning, science and literature.

SOURCE A

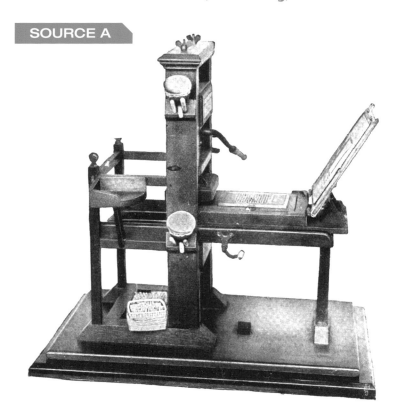

SOURCE B

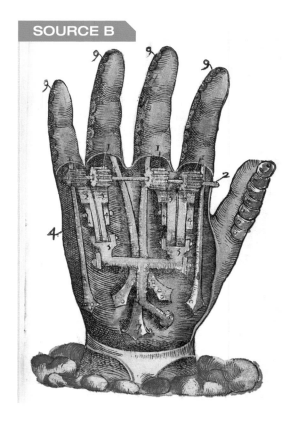

SOURCE C

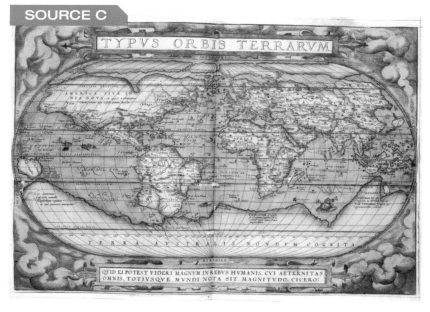

SOURCE D

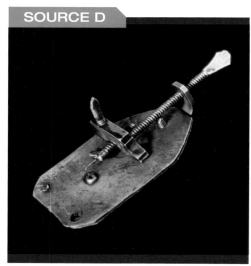

SOURCE E

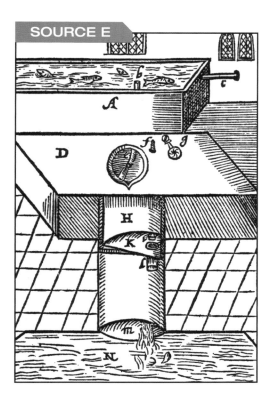

SOURCE F

SOURCE G

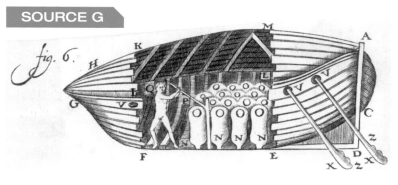

SOURCE H

ACTIVITIES

1 Match one of the captions below to each of the sources here. Each date in the captions shows when we have the first evidence of that invention. It could already have been in use for some years.

Caption	Source, by letter
Microscope, 1595	
False limbs, 1536	
Submarine, 1620	
Flush toilet, 1596	
Seed drill, 1701	
First English printing press, 1478	
Printed maps, 1569	
Telescope, 1608	

2 Colour-code these inventions: political, economic, social, cultural.

3 Explain the significance of each invention.

4 Do these inventions prove that there was a Renaissance?

Pulling things together

From working through this book you will know now that history is about people. These people may have been rulers or ruled, famous or infamous. Anyone in fact, whether their name has been recorded in a history book or not!

On these pages are some of the people you will have met while you have been studying history. Have a look at each picture and caption, then have a go at the activities.

William I, who won the Battle of Hastings

Thomas Becket, who was murdered in Canterbury Cathedral

Wat Tyler, who was leader of the Peasants' Revolt

Henry VIII, who made himself head of the Church in England

Elizabeth I, who ruled England for over 40 years

Francis Drake, who was the first English person to sail around the world

William Shakespeare, who wrote many plays and poems

Guy Fawkes, who tried to kill King James by blowing up Parliament

A witch, who was accused of using magic to harm people

Oliver Cromwell, who was the first commoner to rule England

Charlotte Tremouille, who refused to surrender her home to Parliament's forces during the Civil War

Samuel Pepys, who wrote a diary that tells us about life in seventeenth-century London

Titus Oates, who persuaded many people he had uncovered a Popish plot

Isaac Newton, who was one of the founders of modern science

?

ACTIVITIES

1. Write down the name, or anything you can remember, about people you have studied in history, who are not shown on these pages. Try to do this without checking back in the book first.

2. Write out the list of names in chronological (date) order. Try to do this without checking back in the book first.

3. Write out the names of five people you have studied who you think should be most remembered. Write a sentence or two to explain your choices.

4. Pick two people you have studied, not shown on these pages, who you think really deserve to be remembered.

5. In the last unit you saw how playing cards were often used show important events or people. Produce a set of cards for five people you have studied this year who particularly impress you. You will only have space for five bullet points on each card.

Henry VII
- Reigned 1485–1509
- Became king after killing Richard III at the Battle of Bosworth
- Married Elizabeth of York
- His eldest son, Arthur, died
- Father of Henry VIII

Index